Bhagavan's Song

The Dialogues of Krishna and Arjuna

Translated by
John G. Cunyus
ISBN: 978-1-936497-50-8

© 2025, John G. Cunyus
All Rights Reserved

Searchlight Press
****The Discount Mystic****
"Ancient Wisdom. Texas Twang."
www.JohnCunyus.com
5634 Ledgestone Drive
Dallas, TX. 75214-2026
Peace Peace Peace

"One Teacher,
who is not limited by time,
and that One Teacher
or infinite knowledge,
without beginning or end,
is called God."

Swami Vivekananda

TABLE OF CONTENTS

What Constitutes a Scripture?   7
What are "brahman" and "atman?"   8

The Texas Isha   9

Bhagavan's Song   13

About Bhagavad Gita   13
Who, What, When, Where, Why   15
Arjuna Grieves the Coming Battle   17
    (*Bhagavad Gita* 1:25c, 29-46)
Discourse I   20
    (*Bhagavad Gita* 2:2-3)
Arjuna Restates His Anguish   21
    (*Bhagavad Gita* 2:4-8, 9c)
Discourse II   23
    (*Bhagavad Gita* 2:11-2:53)
Discourse III   30
    (*Bhagavad Gita* 2:54-72)
Discourse IV   33
    (*Bhagavad Gita* 3:3-35)
Discourse V   38
    (*Bhagavad Gita* 3:37-43)
Discourse VI   40
    (*Bhagavad Gita* 4:1-3)
Discourse VII   41
    (*Bhagavad Gita* 4:5-42)
Discourse VIII   47
    (*Bhagavad Gita* 5:2-29)

Discourse IX   52
   (*Bhagavad Gita* 6:1-32)
Discourse X   57
   (*Bhagavad Gita* 6:35-36)
Discourse XI   58
   (*Bhagavad Gita* 6:40-47)
Discourse XII   60
   (*Bhagavad Gita* 7:1-30)
Discourse XIII   65
   (*Bhagavad Gita* 8:3-28)
Discourse XIV   69
   (*Bhagavad Gita* 9:1-34)
Discourse XV   75
   (*Bhagavad Gita* 10:1-11)
Discourse XVI   77
   (*Bhagavad Gita* 10:19-42)
Discourse XVII   81
   (*Bhagavad Gita* 11:5-8)
The Theophany   82
   (*Bhagavad Gita* 11:9-13)
Arjuna's Awestruck Praise   83
   (*Bhagavad Gita* 11:15-31)
Discourse XVIII   86
   (*Bhagavad Gita* 11:32-34)
Arjuna Pleads With Krishna   87
   (*Bhagavad Gita* 11:36-46)
Discourse XIX   90
   (*Bhagavad Gita* 11:47-49)
Discourse XX   91
   (*Bhagavad Gita* 11:52-55)

Discourse XXI	**92**
(*Bhagavad Gita* 12:2-20)	
Discourse XXII	**96**
(*Bhagavad Gita* 13:1-34)	
Discourse XXIII	**102**
(*Bhagavad Gita* 14:1-20)	
Discourse XXIV	**106**
(*Bhagavad Gita* 14:22-27)	
Discourse XXV	**108**
(*Bhagavad Gita* 15:1-20)	
Discourse XXVI	**112**
(*Bhagavad Gita* 16:1-24)	
Discourse XXVII	**116**
(*Bhagavad Gita* 17:2-28)	
Discourse XXVIII	**120**
(*Bhagavad Gita* 18:2-72)	
Arjuna Answers Krishna's Questions	**131**
(*Bhagavad Gita* 18:73)	

Excerpts from ऋग्वेद
Rig Veda   132
The Well-spoken Hymn of Not Non-existence.

Excerpts from उपनिषद्
The Upanishads   134
The Straight Translation of Isha Upanishad

TRANSLATOR'S NOTES   **138**
Various substitutions used for common Sanskrit terms.
Passive Voice and Third-Person Statements
"Stained glass" language.
A Backstory of Arjuna and Krishna
What Does an Italicized Word Mean?
Where Did All the Nicknames Go?

ALSO BY THE AUTHOR   **143**

BOOK DESCRIPTION   **148**

What Constitutes a Scripture?

I hesitated to use the term, "Scripture," as a believing Christian, afraid by using it I would diminish my own Bible and elevate the holy books of others above it.

As a student of religion, however, "Scripture" is easier to classify. A holy book regarded as authoritative in some sense for large groups of religious people through time is a Scripture.

- Among Jews, *Torah* is Scripture, as are *Nevi'im* and *Kethuvim*.
- For Christians, *The Bible* is Scripture, made up of at least the *Old* and *New Testaments*.
- For Muslims, *The Quran* is Scripture, and *The Bible* is highly-regarded.
- For Hindus, *The Vedas* are Scripture, consisting of three layers: the original three Vedas; the *Upanishads*, and *Bhagavad Gita*.

To call these texts *Scriptures* is not to collapse their messages into a single meaning or to flatten their differences. Those are issues for readers to decide. It is to give them a category in our thought to recognize their importance to humanity through the ages.

In that sense, these are excerpts from South Asian Hindu Scriptures.

What are *brahman* and *atman*?

In theistic traditions, reality is understood as dual, divided between God and creation. God is, as theologians say, "wholly present, yet wholly other."

In South Asian understanding, *brahman* is the totality of what theists would call God and creation together. I have left the word untranslated in this text.

Atman is translated as "self." Among its many meanings, it also signifies the reality of *brahman* at the deepest root of embodied beings.

The Texas Isha

Isha Upanishad is the opening chapter of an ancient South Asian holy book. The title means "Sitting at the feet of God." It was written down around 800 years before Christ, after centuries of transmission in oral form, as a chant. "The Texas Isha" puts the ancient work respectfully into a contemporary regional dialect of English. "The Straight Translation," which follows later, is a more literal translation of the ancient Sanskrit document.

Every living speck in this whole mess
is filled by God, down to the quarks.
So, enjoy that you finished some things.
Don't get greedy.
You can't take any of it with you, anyway.
You might live a hundred
years here working hard,
but eventually your work
will come apart.
There are places so dark you can't see a thing.
If you lose sight of who you really are,
that's where you end up.

Just sitting there, it flew faster than the mind;
Even the important ones couldn't catch it
before it soared away.
Just standing there, it outran the runners.
"Breathes-in-the-Mother" puts those waters there.

It moves. It doesn't move.
It's far and near.
It's inside the whole shebang,
and outside it all, too.

Whoever sees all living specks in a Big Self,
and a Big Self in all living specks,
doesn't look down on any of it.
Whoever sees that a Big Self
has become all the living specks.
can't be fooled for long,
and won't grieve forever.
There's a connection.
A Big Self filled it all:
bright, bodiless light, not a mark on it,
not torn by bad stuff.
Self-made for real,
it set the patterns in place forever.

If folks settle down only near worldly ways,
they end up in a very dark place.
If they hang out only near spiritual ways,
they go somewhere even darker.
You get one outcome from being too spiritual,
and another from being too worldly.
We got this from folks who learned it the hard way.
Whoever knows both the spiritual
and the worldly at the same time,
gets past death by the worldly,
and gets to the good place by the spiritual.

Folks who believe in nothing
fall into a very dark place.
Folks who hold on to things
fall into an even darker one.
You get one thing from holding on to things,
and another from believing nothing.
We got this from folks who learned it the hard way.
Whoever knows how things hold together
and how they fall apart,
gets past death through the falling apart,
and gets to the good place through
the holding together.

The way things really are is shut up
behind a locked steel door.
Kick that sucker open!
Let the sunshine in!
We want to see!
You who feed us, see us, kill us, and light us up,
turn your light down! Back away!
That radiant Person from way beyond,
whose form I see in flashes?
That's who I am, too.

The little breath
goes back to the big breath,
and this body turns to dust.
Remember what you've been through!
Remember, Buddy!
Remember what you've been through!

You who burn bright and smart,
drive us down the road to a good place!
Kick the load of bad stuff off us!
We'll keep thanking you when you do.

ईशोपनिषत्
Isha Upanishad 1-18

Bhagavan's Song
Dialogues of
Krishna and Arjuna

Excerpts from
भगवद्गीता
Bhagavad Gita

Bhagavad Gita is a 700-line song, found in the middle of an enormous work of South Asian mythology, *Mahabharata*. This version of the *Gita* excerpts 590 lines of dialogue from the original 700-line poem.

In English, the title means "Bhagavan's Song," or, often, "The Song of God." The title character does most of the singing in the work, accompanied by Arjuna and Sanjaya. Bhagavan's words appear in **red** in this text.

"*Bhaga*," root of the Sanskrit word "Bhagavan," involves **loving**, **partaking**, and **sharing**; and **implies limitless fullness**. Bhagavan is actually a title, rather than a name.

Bhagavad Gita was composed as four-line stanzas in Sanskrit, at some point in the Third Millennium before the Common Era (B.C.E.), in ancient South Asia. It was then passed down orally, in the form of a chant taught to succeeding generations. This process continued for several centuries, at least, before the text was first written down.

The song's lyrics were transliterated at their first writing, rather than translated. Transliteration places spoken words phonetically into an existing alphabet, a process which seems to have taken place between 800 and 400 B.C.E. The alphabet used, *Devanagari*, remains in use today.

The *Devanagari* transliteration itself has been translated many times, into many different languages, through the subsequent millennia. In contrast to transliteration, translation takes words of one language and restates them in another.

You have before you a new translation of a very old song, into a contemporary idiom of English. I hope and pray the Voice of the One speaking may be heard clearly in it.

jgc

Who, What, When, Where, Why

Who: Bhagavan responds to Arjuna's questions. Bhagavan, or Krishna, is represented in the text of *Mahabharata* as an incarnation of God. Arjuna is portrayed as his generation's greatest warrior. Sanjaya, who appears in one segment here, is a later narrator, describing Bhagavan's revelation, to a king named Dhritarashtra.

What: These passages are dialogues between a warrior, Arjuna, and his charioteer, Krishna (Bhagavan), as two armies prepare to battle in a fratricidal civil war. Arjuna, despairing of having to fight against his own family members and mentor, refuses to do battle. Bhagavan counsels him as he considers.

When: In South Asian legend, the events described in *Mahabharata* took place around 3100 B.C.E. In scholarly thought, the document we know as *Bhagavad Gita* took written form between 800 and 400 B.C.E.

Where: The dialogues occur on the battlefield at Kurukshetra, a city in Haryana state, in present-day northwest India.

Why: It is the reader's place to say why.

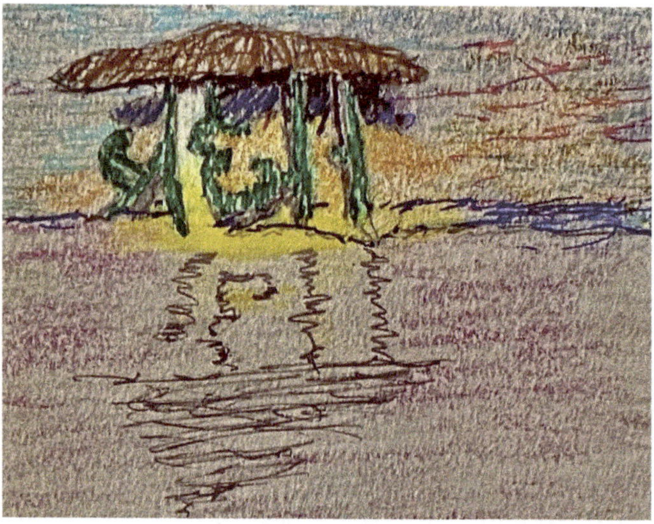

Arjuna Grieves the Coming Battle
Bhagavad Gita 1:25c; 29-46

As the sound of battle grows overwhelming, Arjuna grieves to Bhagavan the terrible deeds the situation demands of him. Bhagavan accompanies Arjuna at Kurukshetra as a non-combatant, armed only with ceremonial weapons, under a vow not to fight. Arjuna begs Bhagavan for the same status. He would rather die, unarmed, than fight and kill those he faces.

[Arjuna} said,
Look! These Kurus
all came together for this.
My limbs sink down,
and my mouth dries up.
My body shakes
and my hair stands on end.
The bow falls from my hand,
and my skin burns.
I can't stand up.
My mind wanders.
I see perverse omens,
and imagine no good fortune
from having killed
my own people in battle.

I don't want victory,
kingship, or pleasure, *O* Krishna.
What good is kingship?
What good are worldly pleasures?

Those we want kingship,
enjoyments, and pleasures for
are ready to fight here,
their lives and wealth abandoned.

Mentors, fathers, sons,
even grandfathers,
mothers' brothers, fathers-in-law, grandsons,
brothers-in-law, relatives —
I don't want to kill them,
though they are killers,
even for *the sake of* rulership
over *the* three worlds —much less for *the* earth!

What joy could it bring us
to strike down Dhritarashtra's sons?
Trouble would follow us
when we've killed these killers.
As I see it, we aren't justified
in killing Dhritarashtra's sons, our kinsmen.
How could we ever be happy again
after killing our own people?

Even if they can't see *the* wrong
caused by destroying *their* family,
or *the* crime of betraying their friends,
even if their mind *is* overpowered by greed;
how could we not see clearly enough
to turn back from this horror,
the wrong caused by destroying family?
We do understand it!

Ancient family laws vanish
when family is destroyed.
When law dies, lawlessness
overwhelms *the* entire family.
When lawlessness overwhelms,
the family's women are raped.
When *the* women are raped,
confusion of duty is born.
This confusion leads to hell.
Even *the* ancestors of
the family-destroyers and *the* family fall,
deprived of *the* living's memory.

The wrongs committed by these
destroyers of family abolish
natural responsibilities and eternal family laws.
I'm confused where my duty lies in this.
We've been taught since childhood
that those whose family laws
are abolished
suffer indefinitely in hell.

What horror! We choose
to do *a* terrible wrong —
to kill our own people,
out of greed for pleasures.
I would be happier
if Dhritarashtra's sons, with weapons in hand,
kill me *instead*,
I'll be unarmed and unresisting.

DISCOURSE ONE
Bhagavad Gita 2:2-3
Bhagavan questions Arjuna's actions.

Bhagavan said,

Where did this fear come from?
It's beneath you.
It won't take you any place worth going,
and people will think it's disgraceful

I know it's not cowardice, Arjuna,
but it still doesn't suit you.
Get up, and put this
wavering behind you.

Arjuna Restates His Anguish
Bhagavad Gita 2:4-8, 9c
Arjuna refuses to fight unless Bhagavan
can clarify the morality of it.

Arjuna said,

>How can I attack
>Bhisma and Drona
>in battle, to kill them?
>They are both revered men.
>
>I'd rather live on earth as *a* beggar
>than kill such noble mentors.
>Can I enjoy earthly pleasures
>*that are* smeared with blood?
>Can I kill my mentors, for worldly gain?
>
>We don't know which is heavier —
>that we conquer, or that they do?
>Would we wish to live
>*when* we've killed the sons of Dhritarashtra
>standing before us?

I'm overwhelmed with pity
and weakness, deep down inside.
I'm asking you. I can't figure out what my duty is.
How can I know what is better? Tell me this!
I'm your disciple, fallen at your feet. Show me!

I can't see how to dispel *this* sorrow,
this drying up of *the* senses,
e*ven if I* attain unrivaled riches and power on earth,
or rulership among *the* gods.

I will not fight

DISCOURSE TWO
Bhagavad Gita 2:11- 2:53
Bhagavan responds to Arjuna's plea.

Bhagavan said,

You're mourning people not to be mourned,
and saying things that seem to be wise but aren't.
The wise don't have to cry over
either *the ones* who *are* gone,
or *the ones who* aren't.
I never was not.
You weren't, either, or any of these other people.
We won't stop existing
in *the* future, either.
The embodied *self* keeps moving
like it does in this body.
It moves through childhood, youth, old age,
and moves to *a* new body after death.
Don't be confused by this.

Cold, heat, happiness, *and* misery
come about from material sensations.
Work to endure them!
They come, they go, they're impermanent.
When these no longer afflict you,
w*hen you're* wise and constant,
in pleasure and pain,
you're ready for immortality.

What isn't real never becomes real.
What is real never stops being so.
When you see truth,
you know both of these are certain.

Understand! *The One* who pervades
all this can't be destroyed.
No one even comes close
to destroying *the* indestructible.
These bodies have *an* end,
but *the* embodied *self*
can't be done away with or measured.
So, fight, *O Arjuna*!

If you think this *one* kills,
and that *one is* killed,
you don't understand.
This doesn't kill, and it isn't killed.
It's never born, and it never dies.
It will never fail to be what it is now.
This primordial *self is* unborn, constant, everlasting.
It is not killed when *a* body is killed.
You know this indestructible,
eternal, and imperishable *One*, even if just *a* little.
How can this deepest self kill?
Who would *it* kill?

As a woman sets aside worn-out clothes,
and puts on newer ones,
the embodied *self* sets aside worn-out bodies,
and puts on newer ones.

Weapons can't pierce it.
Fire can't burn it.
Water won't flood it,
and winds don't dry *it* up.
In fact, it's not to be pierced,
not to be burned,
not to be flooded, not to be dried up.
It can't perish. It pervades all that exists.
It stands firm, immovable, *the* very first.
It's hidden. It's beyond imagining.
Folks say it doesn't change.
Since you understand all this,
you know you don't have to
grieve for these people.

Even if you believed this thing
was born forever or dead forever,
you still don't have to
grieve for these people.
The born will all die,
and *the* dead will all be born.
Because that can't be avoided,
you don't have to grieve for these people.

Living beings are hidden from us
before birth, visible when they're alive,
and invisible again after death.
This is just how things are.
Someone claims they've seen *a* miracle.
Someone else preaches the miracle enthusiastically.
Someone else believes they understand it.

But, they don't know anything.
This embodied *self* can't be hurt
in any body, anywhere.
You, truly, don't have to grieve
for these people, at all.

I know you see *a* terrible duty ahead,
but don't lose heart.
You've found *a* righteous battle, Arjuna.
It's worth putting your whole self into.
A battle like this
opens heaven's door.
Believe it or not,
it's good fortune that you're here.
If you walk away
from this battle now,
no good will come of it.
You'll just trash your own duty and reputation.
People will talk
about your failure forever, too.
For *a* proud man, isn't disgrace
like that worse than death?
The stronger warriors will tell themselves
you wouldn't fight because you were afraid.
After all *the* times they sang your praises,
you'll come to nothing;
Bad people will say things about you
that shouldn't be said.
They'll mock you.
Could there be greater misery?

If they kill *you in battle,*
though, you'll reach heaven.
If you conquer, you'll enjoy earth.
So, get up, Arjuna. *Get* ready to fight!

You've disciplined yourself to deal
with pleasure and pain, gain and loss,
victory and defeat, undisturbed.
Join *the* battle, then, and don't give in to wrong!
Your mentors told you all this in Self-Realization*,
but now's *the* time to put it into practice.
This way, you'll be joined to insight,
and not chained to work.

No effort's lost here.
No one regresses.
Even *a* little discipline
keeps great problems away.
Stay determined
in insight here!
Wavering thoughts meander
all directions, and have no end.

The ignorant proclaim this
with flowery speech:
'*The* love of *the* word of *the* scriptures
is all there is,' they teach.
They're driven by desire, focused on heaven,
promising birth there as *the* outcome of work,
and addicted to all sorts of rituals —
but all of them point to pleasure and authority.

People fixed on pleasure and authority
don't find determined insight in meditation.
Their desire for both
steals their minds away.

Even *the* scriptures belong to three basic drives**.
Let those three drives alone, Arjuna.
Practice being indifferent to polarities,
fixed on eternal truth, not on getting and having,
self-possessed.
The scriptures are as useful
as *a* water well
in *a* flooded field
when someone knows brahman.

Your choice is only *the* work,
not *the* outcome.
Don't let outcome be your motive,
Don't get used to idleness, either.
Do *your* works *with* fixed discipline.
Let go of attachment.
Be *the* same in success or failure.
Equanimity *is a* discipline, *it's* said.
Find peace in insight!
Work doesn't compare
to disciplined intelligence.
People who are in things only for what
they can get out of them *are* sad.

Disciplined intelligence throws off both
good and evil deeds here in this world.

Therefore, join yourself to discipline!
Discipline in works *is a* skill.
The wise, joined to intelligence,
giving up *an* outcome born of works,
freed from *the* bondage of birth,
go to *a* place free from pain.

When your intelligence
finally leaves behind *this* thicket of confusion,
then you go, disgusted with *the* to be heard
and *the* already heard.
When immovable intelligence
steadies itself in deep meditation,
you find discipline.
Stop obsessing over received teaching
that confuses *even the* wise.

*Self-Realization, Samkhya in Sanskrit, is one of the primary schools of ancient South Asian philosophy. It is dualistic, holding to the absolute division between subject and object. The self is pure awareness. Anything the self is aware of is outside itself, an object in awareness. This self is unattached to the objects in its awareness, though it loses that sense of itself in its immersion in the illusion of material existence. The practice of Self-Realization frees individuals from attachment to material nature.

**The three basic drives, *gunas* in Sanskrit, are *tamas* (darkness, inertia), *rajas* (power, force), and *sattva* (light, goodness). Bhagavan analyzes them in depth later in the text.

DISCOURSE THREE
Bhagavad Gita 2:55-72
Arjuna asks what a wise human looks like.

Bhagavan said,

Someone who can let go of
all desires emerging from *the* mind,
a*nd be* content in self by *s*elf,
is said to be steady in insight.
The wise is said to be steady in meditation;
mind free from anxiety in misfortune;
freed from desire in pleasures;
passion, fear, and anger departed.

Someone facing this or that,
pleasant or unpleasant,
steady in all of them,
not rejoicing, not disliking,
is established in this wisdom.
When they withdraw
senses from objects of sense,
like tortoise limbs, completely,
wisdom *is* established.
Sense objects fall away
from *the* fasting of *the* embodied,
except for *the* taste. Even *the* taste
falls away, once you've seen *the* highest.

Even *the* senses
of *the* striving, of wise inner selves,

can forcibly carry away *the* mind,
tearing them.
Better to sit, disciplined,
intent on me, restraining all these,
senses in control,
and wisdom established.

Attachment to sense objects
rises from dwelling on them.
Lust rises from attachment.
Anger rises from lust.
Confusion rises from anger,
and faltering wisdom from confusion.
Faltering wisdom destroys intelligence
When intelligence goes, *the* rest go with it.

When you have self-control, though,
you find peace even when you engage *the* world.
You've freed yourself from passion and hatred
by self-restraint.
All suffering ceases
for someone at peace.
The intelligence of *the* peaceful-minded
steadies itself at once.

There is no intelligence
for *those lacking* discipline,
no meditation for them,
and no peace for them.
Where can their happiness come from?

When thought follows
the wandering senses,
it carries wisdom away with it,
like wind *driving a* boat across water.
Let wisdom be your foundation.
Learn to hold yourself back
from the world you see,
long enough to find peace.
When you are self-restrained,
the self wakes up in what is night to other beings.
What others call "being awake"
will be night to you, perceiving wisdom.

Floods enter *the* ocean,
but *the* ocean doesn't overflow.
Let desires enter you *the* same way.
You'll be the one to find peace,
not *those* who can't stop wanting.
Someone who gives up wanting,
who lives free from lust —
not preoccupied with stuff,
done with making up *an* ego, finds peace.
This is brahman's state.
When you waver in it,
there's still some confusion.
If you stand firm in it, though,
even at *the* point of death,
you reach brahman's light.

DISCOURSE FOUR
Bhagavad Gita 3:3-35
Arjuna asks why Bhagavan urges him to work,
if knowledge is better than work.

Bhagavan said,

I've taught *a* two-fold basis
in this world from of old:
the disciplined knowledge of Self-Realization,
and *the* disciplined works of thorough seekers.

Nobody finds freedom
from work by not working,
and nobody reaches fulfillment
by giving *it* up.
No one ever remains
without work even for *an* instant.
Everyone must work without choice,
by *the* basic drives born of material nature.

Someone who sits there
holding back *the* power of work,
chewing on sense objects in *the* mind,
is *a* hypocrite, with *a* confused mind.
But *someone* doing disciplined work,
controlling senses by mind,
is distinguished by *the* power of work
without attachment.

Do *the* required work — you, yourself!
Work is better than idleness.
Even staying alive in *a* body
can't be done without work.
This world is bound by work,
aside from religious work.
Work for that reason,
free from attachment.

Prajapati, who created humans
alongside religious work, said long ago,
"Bring forth blessings by this.
May this be *the* granting of your desires.
Cause *the* holy to be by this.
Let *the* holy cause you to be.
Reach *the* highest happiness,
causing each other to be.
The holy will give you
the pleasure you desire."

Someone who takes pleasure in
not offering these gifts to *the holy is a* thief.
The good, who share *the* holy table,
are released from all wrongs,
but t*he* wicked eat suffering
when they cook only for themselves.

The living exist by food.
Food exists by rain.
Rain exists by religious work.
Religious work comes about by action.

Know *the* work originating in brahman.
Eternal brahman *is the* source.
All-pervading brahman *is*
established eternally in religious work.
Someone who does not turn *the* wheel
set in motion this way in *the* world,
intending to injure, drunk from sense,
lives in vain.

Yet for someone who delights in self,
contented in self,
pleased in self,
nothing remains to do.
No *hidden* purpose remains
for them here, in work or in idleness;
and no attachment to acquisition for them
among any of *the* living at all.

So, do *the* work to be done,
always, without holding on *to it*!
Working without attachment
is how to attain *the* highest.
Janaka and others after him
found fulfillment by work alone.
Seeing this, your duty is to work
for *the* maintenance of *the* world.
Whatever *the* best people do,
others follow, this and that.
They set *the* standard.
The world follows it.

I have nothing whatever
to accomplish in *the* three worlds,
nothing unattained to be attained —
but I still work.
If I stopped working,
though unwearied,
humans follow my example,
everywhere.
These worlds would die
if I did no work.
I would be *the* maker of chaos,
and destroy these beings.

The unwise are attached to works
as they do them.
Let *the* wise work this way:
without attachment,
intending *only* to keep *the* world going.
Don't fragment *the* minds
of *the* ignorant as they cling to work, though.
You, being wise, keeping discipline,
should cause *them* to enjoy all works.

The basic drives of nature
are doing *the* work in all cases.
Only someone confused by ego-building
thinks, "I am *the* doer."

But *the* knower of truth
having realized this, does not cling.
Basic drives work in basic drives.

Basic drive and work *are* two spheres.
The foolish, confused by *the* basic drives of nature,
hold tight to *those* works, not knowing them whole.
Yet the knower of *the* whole
doesn't need to cause *others* to waver.

Give up all works to me,
meditating on *the* highest self.
Freed from wanting to have,
fever gone — fight!
People who practice
this teaching of mine continually,
full of faith, not mocking —
are set free from works, too.

As for mockers who
won't practice this teaching,
understand them *as* lost, mindless,
confusing all knowledge.
Even *the* wise act
from their own nature.
The living follow nature.
What will subduing *it* accomplish?
Passion and hatred thrive
from senses holding on to *the* objects of sense.
Steer clear of those two.
They aren't your friends.
Better your own duty, unfinished,
than someone else's duty, done well.
An end in your own duty *is* better than
one in someone else's, asking for trouble.

DISCOURSE FIVE
Bhagavad Gita 3:37-43
*Arjuna asks what keeps us from seeing
the divine in real life.*

Bhagavan said,

The basic drive to power
is *the* source of this lust *and* anger.
Understand this adversary here
as devouring and harmful!

The divine, bearing *the* load, is covered by smoke,
like *a* mirror *covered* by dust;
like *a* womb covered by *a* membrane.
Thus, this covered that.
It covers up wisdom.
The perpetual adversary,
with *the* form of lust and unquenchable fire,
hides even *the* wise.
It confuses *the* embodied *self*
by these things, it is said.
The senses, mind, *and* intelligence
of this abode obscure wisdom.
Therefore, mastering *the* senses first,
kill this evil being
w*hich* destroys knowledge
and understanding!

The senses are high, they say.
Mind *is* higher than *the* senses.

Intelligence *is* higher than *the* mind.
This, though, *is* higher than intelligence.
Now that you know
the one higher than intelligence,
who upholds the self by self,
destroy *the* adversary, having *the* form of desire,
difficult to approach!

DISCOURSE SIX
Bhagavad Gita 4:1-3
Bhagavan explains the origin of the teaching.

Bhagavan said,

> I taught this eternal discipline
> to Vivasvat,
> Vivasvat taught Manu.
> Manu passed *it* on to Ishraku.
> In this way, royal seers knew,
> receiving *the* succession.
> This discipline was lost here
> over vast time.
> I teach you
> this ancient discipline today, Arjuna.
> You love me, and *are a* friend,
> *and* this secret teaching is highest.

DISCOURSE SEVEN
Bhagavad Gita 4:4b-42
Arjuna asks Bhagavan how he taught those who died long ago.

Bhagavan said,

>You and I have been born
>many times, Arjuna.
>I remember them all.
>You don't.
>
>Though I am unborn, eternal self,
>though I am *the* Lord of all *the* living,
>I come into material being
>by *my* own supernatural power,
>controlling *my* own nature.
>When doing *the* right decreases,
>*when* lawlessness *and* neglect increase,
>then I offer myself,
>*O* Conqueror of wealth.
>I come into being from age to age,
>to protect *the* righteous,
>to destroy *the* lawless;
>and to establish rightful duty.
>
>Someone who knows
>my divine birth and work,
>does not go to another birth
>when *the* body dies. *They* go to me.

Many reach my state of being,
passion, fear, *and* anger gone,
absorbed in me, focused on me,
cleansed by austere wisdom.
Whatever way they take refuge in me
is *the* way I reward them.
Humans follow my example,
everywhere.

Some sacrifice to gods here,
wanting success in their works.
Some find it quickly
in *this* human world.

I set in motion *a* four-fold division,
according to *the* way basic drives
and works *are* distributed.
Even though I set it in motion,
understand *that my* eternal self *is* beyond all doing.
Works don't defile me.
I have no desire for *the* outcome of work.
Someone who understands me
isn't bound by works, either.
Since you know *the* work
of ancient seekers of liberation,
do *the* work, yourself,
just like they did.

"What work? What idleness?"
Even poets get mixed up here,
so let me explain it to you.

Once you really understand it,
you're freed from wrong.
It's hard to understand
the way work goes —
what you need to know about work,
and about wrong work, and about idleness.
Understand idleness by work,
and work by idleness.
Be disciplined in all work.
That's wisdom, among humans.

The intelligent call someone wise
who keeps lust and *hidden* motive
out of all they do,
and who burns all work in *the* fire of wisdom.
They give up attachment to what comes of work.
They find ways to be content, not dependent.
Even when they are busy,
they're still at peace.
They don't pile up guilt. They don't want too much.
Their mind and self *are* controlled.
They don't grasp. They do what's needed,
without attachment.
They're not bound, even after *the* work is done.
They are content with chance and gain.
They go beyond dualities, free from greed.
They're the same in success and in failure.
The work of *someone* freed from attachment,
liberated, established in wisdom,
working for *a* religious purpose,
melts away entirely.

Brahman *is the* offering, brahman, *the* pouring out,
poured out by brahman, in *the* fire of brahman.
If you contemplate brahman's work,
you'll reach brahman.
Some of *the* disciplined
offer religious work to *the* divine.
Others offer religious work,
by *the* same act, in *the* fire of brahman.
Others offer senses *and* hearing,
in *the* fires of restraint.
Others offer objects of sense *and* sound,
in *the* fires of *the* senses.
Still others offer all sense actions,
even breathing,
in *the* fire of self-discipline,
kindled by wisdom.

Some offer material possessions, austerity,
and discipline, as religious work.
Some are ascetics, sharpened by vows,
whose religious works are
scripture study and wisdom.
Others offer in this way:
the inhaled breath exhaling,
and *the* exhaled breath inhaling;
restraining *the* paths of inhaling and exhaling;
intent on controlling *the* breath.
Others, who've been restrained in food,
offer breaths into breaths.
All these understand religious work.

Their wrongs are destroyed, through religious work.
They go to primordial brahman,
enjoying *the* sweetness left over
from religious work.
This world isn't for those who reject religious work.
How could *the* next *one be*?

Accordingly, understand many kinds
of religious works, all arising from brahman.
Knowing this, speaking and living it,
all *those* born of work will be freed.
Offering wisdom is better than
offering material possessions.
Wisdom fully contains
all work.
Learn this by submitting carefully,
by asking thoughtful questions, *and* by serving.
Knowers and seers of truth
will teach you wisdom.
Once you know this,
you will see all *the* living
in yourself, *and* then in me.
You won't fall into confusion again.

Even if you *were the* wickedest
of all *the* wicked,
you'll get through all of it
on *the* boat of wisdom.
A kindled fire turns
firewood to ashes, *O* Arjuna;

and wisdom's fire turns
all works to ashes.
There is no purifier
like wisdom in this world.
When you master discipline,
you find yourself in *the* self in time.
You reach wisdom when you're full of faith,
devoted to it, senses restrained.
When you reach wisdom,
you're close to *the* highest peace.
An ignorant, faithless,
and doubting self is lost.
There is no happiness for *a* doubting self,
in this world or beyond it.

Works do not bind some*one*
who renounces work, in discipline.
For the self-possessed,
wisdom severs *their* doubt.
Therefore, cut away this doubt in *the* heart!
Use wisdom's sword in yourself!
Get up from ignorance! Go to discipline!
Rise up!

DISCOURSE EIGHT
Bhagavad Gita 5:2-29
Arjuna asks Bhagavan which is better:
renunciation or disciplined work.

Bhagavan said,

>Renunciation and disciplined work
both lead to *the* highest happiness.
Of *the* two, disciplined work
is better than renunciation.
Someone deserves to be called a renunciate,
who neither hates nor desires,
indifferent to polarities,
freed pleasantly from bondage.

>*The* foolish say Self-Realization and discipline
are distinct, not those who know better.
You find *the* outcome of both
when even one *is* done right.
Disciplined workers find *the* same place
followers of Self-Realization do.
Someone who sees this, sees that
Self-Realization and discipline *are* one.

>I'm telling you, renunciation *is*
painful without discipline.
Joined to discipline, though,
the self-disciplined reach brahman quickly.
Someone joined to discipline, self cleansed,
self pacified, senses controlled,

. whose self has become *the* self of all *the* living,
isn't polluted, even when they act.
The steadfast knower of truth thinks,
"I do nothing at all:
seeing, hearing, touching, smelling,
eating, walking, sleeping, breathing;
speaking, shitting, grabbing,
even opening and shutting *the* eyes."

They are convinced of this:
senses abide in objects of senses.
Someone who acts, laying everything down
on brahman, attachment abandoned,
isn't polluted by evil,
like *a* lotus leaf *isn't* by water.
The disciplined work for self-purification
by body, mind, intelligence,
and even merely by *the* senses,
letting go instead of holding tight.
The disciplined *person* lets go
of *a* work's outcome, *and* reaches *a* steady peace.
The undisciplined, driven by want,
holding tight to *a longed-for* outcome, is bound.
Renouncing all works in mind,
the embodied *one* sits happily *as* ruler
in *the* nine-gated city*,
neither acting nor causing to act.

The Lord creates neither *the* state of action
nor *the* work of *the* world,
nor *the* joining together of work and outcome.

Nature, on *the* other hand, does.
The All-pervading does not receive
either *the* wickedness or *the* virtue of anyone.
Ignorance conceals knowledge,
and *the* living are confused by it.

Yet knowledge of self
destroys this ignorance.
Then, highest wisdom
shines like *the S*un.
Those whose intelligence
is absorbed in *brahman*,
whose selves *are* fixed on it,
who lay their foundation *on it*,
who hold it as *the* highest good,
do not go again to rebirth,
wrongs shaken off by wisdom.
The wise see *the* same *self*
in *a* priest endowed with knowledge and training,
in *an* elephant, in *a* dog,
and *even* in *a* cooker of dogs.

Brahman *is* without evil *and* unchanging,
for those who've conquered birth here,
whose minds are steady in equanimity,
They are established in brahman.
Brahman's knowers, established in brahman,
intelligence firm, not confused,
don't need to rejoice getting what they want,
or shudder getting what they don't.

Someone not holding tight to sensual stimulation,
a self who finds happiness in *the* self,
joined in discipline to brahman,
reaches *an* imperishable happiness.

Pleasures born of sensations
give birth to suffering.
The intelligent aren't content in them,
because all sensations have *a* beginning and *an* end.
If you learn to endure *the* agitation
born of lust and anger here in this life,
before liberation from *the* body,
y*ou'll be* disciplined *and* happy.
When happiness *and* delight *are* within,
you also *have* radiance within.
Practicing discipline, absorbed in brahman,
you reach brahman's light,

Seers whose wrongs are destroyed
attain brahman's light,
dualities cut away, selves restrained,
content in *the* welfare of all being.
Brahman's light is near
for those who've let go of anger and desire,
for *the* austere, those whose thoughts are governed,
for those who know *the* self.
Sensory pleasures pushed aside,
inner gaze focused between *the* two eyebrows,
inhaling and exhaling equal,
and moving within *the* nose;
sense, mind, *and* intelligence *are* controlled,

aiming for liberation.
Lust, fear, and anger *have* vanished.
These *people* are liberated always.

Sages reach peace
once they've known me.
I am the companion of all being.
I find *the* joy *in every* offering of austerity.

*The "nine-gated city" is the human body; its nine "gates" are two eyes, two ears, two nostrils, one mouth, one opening for excretion, and one for procreation.

DISCOURSE NINE
Bhagavad Gita 6:1-31
*Bhagavan describes for Arjuna
the practice of discipline.*

Bhagavan said,

If you do *the* work you need to,
not hung up on *the* outcome of it,
you are *the* renunciate and *the* disciplined.
It's not about just giving up rites and rituals.
Know *the kind of* renunciation
they call discipline.
No one gets discipline
without giving up lust.
Someone rises to discipline
by *a* simple method: work.
Someone who has risen to discipline
keeps it by *a* simple method: calm.
When someone stops holding tight
to sensual desires, or to work,
giving up every ulterior motive,
others say they've risen to discipline.

Lift up yourself by self.
Don't degrade yourself.
Self can *be the* friend of self.
Self can *be the* enemy of self.
Self is *a* friend to those
who've overcome self by self.

An unmastered self can be
a hostile enemy.
The highest self of *the* peaceful
who've mastered self, makes steady:
in cold *and* heat, pleasure *and* misery,
as well as in honor and dishonor.

You're disciplined
when you understand that wisdom is enough;
when you don't change
whichever way the wind blows;
when you don't give in to *the* wandering senses.
Mud, stone, gold — what's the difference?
No more undue affection, nor more hatred,
for friend, companion, *even* enemy;
finding *a* middle ground between
adversaries and loved ones alike;
judgment withheld between
what's reputed to be wrong and right.
It's a good perspective when you get there.

You *are* disciplined.
Now, concentrate yourself in self.
Stay in solitude. Keep hold of thought and self.
Let go of wanting and having.
Sit down in *an* unpolluted spot,
not too high, not too low.
Cover it with cloth,
soft grass, and fragrant flowers.
Direct *your* mind to *a* single point,
Watch thought and sense.

Practice discipline to purify yourself,
sitting right there;
Keep body, head, *and* neck erect;
holding still, not moving;
focusing eyes on *the* tip of *the* nose;
and not looking around.
Just sit, mind pacified, disciplined,
self made peaceful, fear banished,
established in *a* vow of continence,
intent on me, loving me.

The disciplined *keep* mind restrained,
concentrating continually in self.
They go to peace, to *the* highest light,
and find communion with me.
Discipline isn't eating too much,
or just fasting from food.
It doesn't come from sleeping too much,
or trying to stay awake.
W*hen* we're disciplined in food and pleasure;
disciplined in doing works;
and disciplined in sleeping and being awake,
discipline destroys suffering.

Someone absorbed in self,
thought pacified,
free from longing, free from lust,
is said to be steady.
Like *a* candle in *a* windless place
that does not flicker,
so *is the* thought of *the* disciplined,

focused on self-discipline.
Spend time where thought is at rest,
restrained by disciplined practice,
and where self is content,
seeing self by self;
where you know *the* joy
by which fixed intelligence
goes beyond *the* senses.
The wise don't wander away from what is true.
Once you attain it, you stop dreaming about
unreal pleasures always just beyond reach.
Rooted there, you don't have to be shaken,
even in profound sorrow.

Call this dissolving
of *the* union with sorrow, discipline.
Practice this discipline,
not feeling sorry for yourself;
motives not rising from lusts,
wantings entirely given up by *the* mind,
obsession with sensual pleasures
wholly overcome.

Little by little, learn to be quiet,
grasped firmly by intelligence.
Let *the* mind stand firmly in self,
considering nothing else at all.
When *the* mind wanders away,
flitting here and there, unfixed,
bring it back, restraining
mind in self.

Highest happiness itself comes near
the disciplined, *the* peaceful in mind,
emotion pacified, free of evil,
united with brahman.
Practicing discipline regularly in self,
freed from wrong, *the* disciplined
attains boundless happiness:
contact with brahman.

Join *yourself* to discipline.
See self present in all *the* living,
and all *the* living *present* in self.
Watch *it all* equally at all times.
When you see me everywhere,
and see all in me,
I am not lost to you,
and you aren't lost to me.
When you, self-disciplined,
firmly one *with me*,
honor me *as I* abide in all *the* living,
you live in me, whatever way you turn.
Self-discipline people,
living life with equanimity
in pleasure or pain —
could that be *the* highest *state*?

DISCOURSE TEN
Bhagavad Gita 6:35-36
*Arjuna asks how such practice is possible
for an unsteady mind.*

Bhagavan said,

>It's hard to tame *a* restless mind.
>It only happens by practice,
>You have to turn away
>from much that *the* world wants.
>I see it like this:
>you can't reach discipline
>without self-control.
>You can *only* reach it by practice.

DISCOURSE ELEVEN
Bhagavad Gita 6:40-47
*Arjuna asks if those unable
to steady the mind are lost?*

Bhagavan said,

> I don't lose anybody
> here or hereafter.
> Hear me, Arjuna.
> Nothing good is lost.
> If you tried, and failed,
> I'll remember your effort for *the* good.
> When you've had time to recover,
> I'll give you another chance.
>
> Sometimes, someone's born
> in *a* self-disciplined family.
> They may not appreciate it all *the* time,
> but they'll understand *the* blessing eventually.
> You'll get to start over,
> but you'll do it
> with all *the* wisdom
> you earned before.
> That wisdom, present there
> because of someone's prior practice,
> will carry you forward —
> sometimes kicking and screaming —
> but brahman won't be idle talk to you.

Disciplined, self-controlled;
made clean from wrong by hard work;
made whole, *through* starting over many times;
you go from there to *the* highest goal.
Being disciplined is more than just giving things up.
It's the best education available,
better than making a show of religion.
Be disciplined, Arjuna!

Of all *the* disciplined people around, too,
it's those who actually love,
whose inner lives fill with faith,
who are *the* steadiest. So folks say.

DISCOURSE TWELVE
Bhagavad Gita 7:1-30
Bhagavan explains wisdom to Arjuna.

Bhagavan said,

This is how you know
whose mind is absorbed in me:
they practice discipline; they find refuge in me;
they're complete in me, without doubt.
I will explain wisdom to you,
full understanding.
Once you understand it, there's nothing more
that has to be added, here or hereafter.
Hardly one in a thousand
works toward communion in this life.
Hardly any, even of *those,*
know me in reality.

I divided nature into eight parts:
earth, waters, fire, wind,
sky, mind, intelligence,
and even *the* making of *an* I.
All this comes from me.
This is *a* lower *part*, but know
my other, higher nature:
spiritual beings, by which
this universe is sustained.

Understand this.
All *the* living begin in this.

I *am the* origin and dissolution
of *the* entire universe.
Nothing else
is greater than me.
These *worlds are* all strung on me
like pearls on *a* thread.
I'm liquidity in waters.
I'm *the* radiance that contains sun and moon,
the sacred syllable in all scriptures.
I'm sound in air, fertility among humans.
I'm *the* pure fragrance of *the* earth,
and *the* brilliance of *the* sun.
I'm life in all *the* living,
and self-denial among ascetics.

Know me *as*
the primordial seed of all *the* living.
I'm *the* intelligence of *the* intelligent,
and the brilliance of *the* brilliant.
I'm *the* strength of *the* strong,
freed from passion and lust.
I am love in all *the* living,
consistent with law,

Know *that the* basic drives —
darkness, power, and **light** —
are in me. I am not in them,
but they are in me.
Confused by *these* three basic drives,
not all of this world
recognizes me a*s* eternal,

as higher than these.
I spin this divine illusion,
hard to penetrate, from *the* drives *themselves*.
But if you'll turn only to me,
you'll go beyond *the* illusion.

The lowest among us, confused,
don't take refuge in me.
The illusion takes away their wisdom,
because they're holding on to lesser things.

Four types of benevolent people
honor me, *O* Arjuna:
the afflicted; *those* seeking wisdom;
those wanting *the* highest truth;
and *the* wise.
The wise stands out among them,
joined to discipline, loving one alone.
I don't just love *the* wise. I enjoy them, as well,
and they enjoy me.
All of them are noble,
but *the* wise *are* like my very self.
They are steady, a*nd they* abide in me.
I am the highest goal.
At *the* end of many births,
the wise take refuge in me,
confessing, "Vasudeva* is all!"
Such great selves *are* hard to find.

Others take refuge in other gods,
stripped of wisdom by various lusts,

practicing various religious obligations,
worn down by their own nature.
I myself grant
immovable faith
to whoever faithfully longs
to worship whatever form.
Someone, joined to such faith,
who longs to find forgiveness by it,
finds it there.
I answer such determined longing.
But *the* outcome is fleeting
for *the* small-minded.
Still, those worshiping gods go to *the* gods.
Those worshiping me surely go to me.

The unintelligent think I've fallen
into *the* visible, though *I am* invisible,
They don't know my higher being,
which is eternal *and* incomparable.
I'm not visible to all,
concealed by *the* illusion of my discipline.
This confused world does not recognize me,
unborn, eternal.
Yet I know *those who've*
crossed over, *those still* living,
and *those* yet to be.
Still, no one knows me.

The rising up of lust and loathing,
and *the* misunderstanding of dualities,

drive all *the* living to confusion
at birth.
People whose actions are pure,
whose wickedness has come to *an* end,
freed from duality and confusion,
worship me with firm vows.
Those who work relentlessly
for release from old age and dying,
come to know brahman, *the* highest self, and work,
in total, and without gap.
Those who know me as *the* highest being,
the highest God, and *the* basis of religious work,
their thoughts steady, also know me
even at *the* time of death.

* Vasudeva, meaning "shining god," is one of Bhagavan's many titles.

DISCOURSE THIRTEEN
Bhagavad Gita 8:3-28
Arjuna asks what brahman and the highest self are.

Bhagavan said,

Brahman *is the* highest, *the* eternal.
The highest self, it's said,
is *the* origin of being.
The creative power is called work.
The highest being *is* perishable existence,
the highest Human *is the* highest God,
and I *am the* basis of religious work
in this world.
When you remember me at *the* time of death,
letting go of *the* corpse,
you attain my state of being.
In this case, there's no doubt.

Pay attention to this, though.
You will go to whatever impulses
fill your heart at *the* time of death.
That's what you'll become.
Remember me, then,
at all times, and fight.
Fix mind and intelligence on me!
You will surely reach me.
You go, meditating,
to *the* highest divine Human,
by practicing discipline,
and allowing thought to go nowhere else.

Remember *the* poet, *the* ancient ruler,
subtler than *an* atom, yet *the* foundation of all;
whose form *is* inconceivable,
whose color *is* that of *the* Sun, beyond darkness.
Mind stilled at *the* time of departure,
joined with love, disciplined with strength,
having caused life's breath to enter correctly
between *the* two eyebrows,
you go to *the* divine highest Human.

Let me explain that path to you, briefly.
Those knowing scripture call *it* eternal.
The austere enter it, free from passion,
loving it so highly they give up all else.
Controlling all *the* body's gates,
confining mind in heart,
self's vital breath placed in *the* head,
firm in disciplined concentration,
speaking *the* sacred syllable, Oṁ,
meditating on me, brahman,
go forth, renouncing *the* body.
You will reach *the* highest path.
I'm easy to reach, Arjuna,
when your mind doesn't wander,
when you remember me continually,
when you are joined to me and disciplined.
Great selves, coming to me,
having touched *the* highest fulfillment,
don't incur rebirth, *which is a*
home of misery *and* impermanence.

Worlds up to *the* creator's realm
are subject to successive rebirths,
but those approaching me
aren't reborn.
They know *the* creator's day,
lasting *a* thousand ages;
and *the* night, ending *a* thousand ages.
They know both day and night.
All manifestations from *the* invisible
originate at daybreak.
They dissolve again there at nightfall,
invisible again.
This multitude of *the* living,
having come into being again and again,
is dissolved inevitably at nightfall.
It comes into being at daybreak.

But *an* invisible state of being,
higher than this other, endures,
which does not perish
in *the* perishing of all *the* living.
Invisible, eternal, thus said —
they call this *the* highest path.
When you reach it, you don't have to come back.
This is my highest dwelling place.
This is *the* highest Human,
reachable by love, but not directed by it elsewhere.
All *the* living exist within it,
and it pervades them all.

Let me tell of the moment,
when *the* disciplined depart in time,
going, turning back,
and not turned back.
If those knowing brahman depart
in fire, brightness, day, *the* bright lunar fortnight,
the northern six-month phase of *the* sun,
they attain brahman.
If the disciplined depart during
smoke, night, *the* dark lunar fortnight,
the southern six-month phase of *the* sun,
they attain *the* lunar brightness, and return to birth.
These two paths, light and dark,
are thought to be eternal.
One leads to non-return,
and the other leads back to birth again.

You know these two paths.
Let there be no confusion in your practice.
Join yourself to discipline
at all times.
By steady practice, *you* go beyond rebirth,
to *the* highest primal abode. You understand all this,
through scriptures, religious works, and austerity;
a*nd* through gifts which ordained *a* pure outcome.

DISCOURSE FOURTEEN
Bhagavad Gita 9:1-34
Bhagavan explains secret wisdom to Arjuna.

Bhagavan said,

Let me explain this secret to you,
since you aren't *a* mocker.
Wisdom and understanding go together.
Once you understand, you're free from impurity.
This is *the* highest knowledge,
fit even for *the* powerful. It purifies,
and is easy to grasp. It breaks no law,
is satisfying to practice, and it doesn't disappear.
People without faith
in this law don't reach me.
They are reborn
in *the* path of death and rebirth.

I fill this whole universe
with my unseen presence.
All *the* living abide in me,
but I don't abide in them.
Understand, though! This is
my highest discipline: that *the* living
do not abide in me. *I* uphold *the* living.
The living do not uphold me.
I cause *the* living to be by m*y very* self.
Like *the* mighty wind that lives in space,
forever going wherever it will,
all *the* living live in me.

Practice seeing it this way.

All *the* living return to my nature
at *the* end of *the* creator's day.
I send them out again
at *the* beginning of *the* next.
I create again and again, of my own will,
this entire material universe,
devoid of its own choice,
supported by my own nature.
These works
don't bind me.
I watch them like *a* bystander,
unconcerned with outcomes.
Nature creates,
animate and inanimate.
I look on, as witness.
The universe revolves from this.

The confused despise me
taking human form.
They can't see my higher being,
the great Lord of *the* living.
Unfortunately, their hopes and actions
lead nowhere. Their wisdom,
if you can call it that, is futile, senseless,
scheming, even wicked.
That's what results from *a* confused character.

Great selves, though,
make *a* home in *the* divine nature.

They worship, not distracted, knowing
the eternal origin of *the* living.
Be steady. Worship.
Celebrate *the* wonder,
keeping sincere promises,
and honoring me with love.

Others may honor me as one, or as many.
Their worship might be
religious works of wisdom,
I make myself manifest variously,
facing all directions.
I *am the* ceremony, *and* I *am the* religious work.
I *am the* offering, *and* I *am the* herb.
I *am* holy words repeated,
and I *am the* clarified butter.
I *am the* fire, *and* I *am the* pouring out.
I *am the* father of this universe,
the mother, *the* founder, *the* grandfather,
the to be known, *the* purifier, *the* syllable *Oṁ*,
the Rig, Sama, and Yajur *Vedas*.
I am the goal, *the* sustainer,
the great Lord, *the* eyewitness,
the home, *the* refuge, *the* good companion,
the origin, *the* dissolution, *the* basis,
the treasure house, *the* eternal seed.
I radiate heat. I hold back
and let loose rain.
I am immortality and death,
being and non-being.

Knowers of scripture, ritual purists, cleansed of evil,
worshiping me with religious works, want heaven.
They reach *the* holy world of *the* gods' king,
and enjoy divine, godly pleasures in *the* sky.
But after they've enjoyed heaven,
after they've spent their merit,
they come back to this mortal world.
This confirms *the* scriptures.
They want one outcome,
but what they get comes and goes.

I lead people who worship me
to getting and having *what they want,*
when they direct their thoughts
consistently, joined to discipline.
Even *the ones* worshiping
other gods in good faith
come to me, though they don't
worship according to rule.
I am *the* enjoyer and Lord
of all religious works,
but they don't know me in reality.
That's why they fall.
Those devoted to gods reach *the* gods.
Those devoted to ancestors reach *the* ancestors.
Those offering to *the* living reach *the* living.
Those making offerings to me reach me.
If you offer me *a* leaf,
a flower, fruit, *or* water, with love,
I accept that offering of love
from *a* pure self.

Offer me
whatever you do, whatever you eat,
whatever you set out, whatever you give,
whatever you practice.
This is how you'll be freed from *the* chains of work,
from both good and evil outcomes.
You'll come to me,
joined to *the* discipline of renunciation.

I *am the* same in all *the* living.
I neither favor nor disfavor any.
But I *am near* those who honor me
with love, and they *are near* in me.
I consider even wrong-doers righteous
when they honor me,
and love no other.
They made *the* right resolution.
They grow quickly in holiness,
and enter everlasting peace.

Understand this:
no one who loves me is lost.
Those who take refuge in me,
reach *the* highest goal,
even if they come from *the* wrong places;
even if they're women, or traders, or laborers.
How much more holy pilgrims,
and loving seekers!

Since you've come to this impermanent,
unhappy world, devote yourself to me.
Be one whose mind is fixed on me.
Worship. Do religious work. Make reverence.
In this way, joined to discipline, with me as
the highest goal, you'll come to me — *the s*elf.

DISCOURSE FIFTEEN
Bhagavad Gita 10:1-11
*Bhagavan restates the highest word,
desiring to bless the hearer.*

Bhagavan said,

Listen to me again, Arjuna.
I'll repeat this highest word another time,
because I love you
and want your well-being.
All those gods and great seers together
don't know my origin.
I *am the* source of
all gods and of great seers.
When you know me as birthless
and beginningless, *the* world's great Lord,
that's *a* clarity most of *the* death-bound never find.
It frees *you* from all wrongs.

Intelligence, wisdom, clarity,
patience, truthfulness, self-restraint, equanimity,
pleasure, pain, being, non-being,
fear, and even fearlessness;
non-violence, impartiality, contentment,
austerity, benevolence, repute, disrepute —
the conditions of being arise
in their many forms from me.

Seven great seers in previous times,
a*nd* four human ancestors

were born from mind, originating in me.
The world and these creatures come from this.
When you know my visible power
and discipline, you join me,
with unwavering self-control.
There is no doubt of this.

I *am the* origin of all.
All begins from me.
You honor me in your intelligence
by thinking this way, endowed with meditation.
Those who think of me, who concentrate
breath on me, awakening each other
and speaking continually of me,
are content and find joy.

I give *to the* disciplined,
constant in practice, worshiping in kindness,
the intelligence by which
they come to know me.
If some are moved to compassion,
by wisdom's bright light,
I cause *the* ignorance born of darkness
to be destroyed inside them.

DISCOURSE SIXTEEN
Bhagavad Gita 10:19-42
Arjuna asks Bhagavan how he may be known.

Bhagavan said,

>Listen! I'll tell you
my most prominent
divine self manifestations,
but there is no end to my extent.
I am *the* self, dwelling
in *the* resting place of all being.
I am *the* beginning and *the* middle
of all *the* living, and *the* end as well.

>I am Vishnu among *the* Adityas,
the radiant Sun among lights.
I am Marici among storm gods.
I am *the* Moon among nightly lights.
I am Sama among *the* Vedas.
I am Vasuva among gods,
and I am *the* mind among *the* senses.
I am consciousness among *the* living.

>I am Shiva among *the* forces
of destruction and renewal,
the Lord of wealth among Yaksas and Raksas.
I am flame among *the* Vasus.
I am Meru among mountains.
Know me to be chief among
household priests, *the* priest of *the* gods.

I am *the* god of war among commanders of armies.
I am *the* ocean among bodies of water.
I am Bhrigu among *the* great seers.
I am *the* one syllable among sayings.
I am *the* whispered prayer among religious works,
and the abode of snow among immovables.

I am the sacred fig among all trees,
Narada among divine seers,
'He whose chariot is bright'
among heavenly musicians,
a*nd* Kapila *the* sage among *the* fulfilled.
Know me *as* Ucchaisravas
among horses, *as* born of nectar,
as Airavata among princely elephants,
and *as the* great Lord among humans.
I *am the* thunderbolt among weapons
and *the* Cow of Plenty among cows.
I *am the* god of love procreating
and I am Vasuki among serpents.
I am Ananta among snakes,
I am Varuna among sea monsters,
and I am Aryanam among *the* ancestors.
I am *the* god of Death among subduers.

I am Prahlada among *the* Daityams,
I am Time among *the* reckoners,
I am *the* King of Beasts among beasts,
and Garuda among birds.
I am *the* wind among purifiers,
I am Rama among those bearing weapons,

I am Makara among crocodiles,
and I am *the* Ganges among rivers.

I am *the* beginning and *the* end
among creations, and *the* middle.
I am knowledge of *the* highest self
among fields of study,
and discourse among those who speak.
I am *the* letter A among *the* indestructibles,
and *the* simple compound among compound *words*.
I alone am infinite Time.
I am *the* founder, facing in all directions.

I am all-destroying death,
and *the* origin of those that are to be.
I am fame, wealth, and speech,
among womanly words,
memory, mental vigor, courage, *and* patience.
I am *the* Brihatsman among chants,
and Gayatri among poetic meters.
I am Marga-sirsa among months,
and Spring, abounding with flowers,
among seasons.

I *am the* gambling of cheats.
I *am the* brilliance of *the* brilliant.
I *am* victory. I *am* effort.
I *am the* goodness of *the* good.
I am Vasudeva among *the* Vrishnis,
and the Conqueror of Wealth among Pandu's sons.

I am Vyasa* among sages,
and Usana *the* poet among poets.

I am clout among rulers,
I am guidance among seekers of victory,
and I am silence among secrets.
I am wisdom among *the* wise.
I am also that which *is the* seed
among all *the* living, *O* Arjuna.
Nothing could exist without me,
animate or inanimate.

There is no end
to my divine manifestations,
but I declare them to this extent,
by way of explanation.
Understand about me, you yourself!
Whatever brilliant, glorious,
and powerful truth *exists*, indeed,
originates from *a* fraction of *this* brilliance.
However, what *is* this extensive
knowledge to you?
I support this entire universe
continually, by *a* single fraction.

*Vyasa, mentioned here, was thought traditionally to be ***Bhagavad Gita***'s original composer.

DISCOURSE SEVENTEEN
Bhagavad Gita 11:5-8
Arjuna asks Bhagavan to show him His glory.

Bhagavan said,

> See *my* various divine forms,
> *a* hundred fold,
> rather, *a* thousand fold,
> and multiple colors and shapes.
> See Adityas, Vasus, Rudras,
> two Asvins, Maruts as well!
> See many wonders
> unseen before.
> See *the* entire universe, gathered
> as one today, with everything
> — animate and inanimate — in *my* body,
> and whatever else you desire to see!
>
> But you are not able
> to see me with your own eye.
> I give you *the* divine eye.
> See this majestic discipline!

The Theophany
Bhagavad Gita 11:9-13
Sanjaya, the narrator,
describes Bhagavan's revelation to Arjuna.

Sanjaya said,

>Having spoken thus, then, O King,
>*the* mighty Lord of discipline
>revealed to Partha
>*his* sublime highest form:
>not merely one mouth or eye,
>not merely one wondrous sight,
>not merely one divine ornament,
>not merely one raised, divine weapon;
>wearing divine garlands and garments,
>bearing divine scent and ointment —
>God, made of all wonder,
>infinite, facing all directions.

>Should *the* brilliance of *a* thousand suns
>rise in *the* sky all at once,
>thus might *the* brightness
>of this great self be.
>Pandava saw there
>*the* entire universe, gathered as one,
>in *the* body of *the* God of gods,
>in no way divided.

Arjuna's Awestruck Praise
Bhagavad Gita 11:15-31
Arjuna reacts to the divine appearance.

Arjuna said,

I see gods in your body, *O* God,
all species of *the* living, together.
I see the creator Lord sitting on *a* lotus throne,
seers, and all heavenly earth-goers.
I see your unending form in every direction —
not merely one arm, belly, face, or eye.
Moreover, I see of you
not *an* end, not *a* middle, and not yet *a* beginning,
O Lord of all, whose form is *the* universe.

I see you, who are difficult to behold completely,
crowned, armed with *a* club, carrying *a* discus,
a mass of brilliance, shining in all directions,
the radiance of Sun and flaming fire,
beyond measure:
you, *the* highest imperishable to be known;
you, *the* highest resting place of all this;
you, *the* eternal defender of righteousness;
you, *the* primordial Human, by my understanding.
Without beginning, middle, or end,
infinite *in* power, having innumerable limbs,
holder of Sun and Moon as eyes —
I see you, mouth blazing, consuming *the* offering,
lighting up all this universe
with your own brilliance.

You alone fill all this
between heaven and earth, on all sides.

The three worlds shake, *O* great self,
having seen your wondrous, terrifying form.
Over there, throngs of gods enter you.
Some, terrified, praise with reverent gestures.
Crowds of seers and *the* fulfilled praise you
with overflowing praises, saying "Hail!"
Rudras, Adityas, Vasus, and Sadhyas,
Visve gods, two Asvins, Maruts,
and *the* steam drinkers,
throngs of Gandharvas, Asuras,
and completed beings
all see you, overcome by amazement.

Worlds *are* shaking, as am I,
having seen your great form —
many mouths and eyes, many arms,
many thighs and feet, many bellies,
many tusks.
Having seen you, I tremble in *the* inner self.
I find neither courage nor calm, *O* Vishnu —
watching you touching *the* blazing sky, many-
colored, mouth gaping, eye burning, enormous.
Having seen your mouth,
like *the* fires of time, bearing many tusks,
I don't know *the* direction, and I find no comfort.

Have mercy, Lord of gods, abode of *the* universe!
From there, Dhritarashtra's sons enter you,

along with all *the* throng of world rulers;
Bhisma, Drona, *the* charioteer's son,
together with our chief warriors also.
They quickly enter your
fearsome mouth, gaping with tusks.
I see their crushed skulls,
stuck between your teeth.
As many torrents of water
flow on to *the* ocean,
so these world-famous heroes
enter your blazing mouths.
As moths enter *a* roaring flame
with great speed, to destruction,
so *the* worlds enter your mouths,
with great speed, to destruction.

You lick, devouring all *the* worlds
on all sides, your mouths blazing.
Your fierce radiance, *O* Vishnu, filling all
with brilliance, consumes *the* universe.
Tell me who you are, *you* of terrifying form!
Reverence to you, *O* Best of Gods!
Have mercy! I wish to understand you.
Truly, I don't comprehend your purpose.

DISCOURSE EIGHTEEN
Bhagavad Gita 11:32-34
*Bhagavan clarifies the terrifying vision
Arjuna has seen.*

Bhagavan said,

I am mighty Time, destroyer of *the* world,
come forth to bring *the* worlds here to nothing.
The soldiers arrayed here
in opposing armies for battle
will not continue in this form, even without you.

Therefore, stand up, you yourself! Attain glory!
Enjoy prosperous kingship,
having conquered enemies!
I have destroyed these already.

Be *the* mere instrument!
You yourself kill these warrior heroes
slain by me: Drona, and Bhisma, and Jayadratha,
Karna, also, and others! Don't hesitate!
Fight! You will conquer enemies in battle.

Arjuna Pleads with Krishna
Bhagavad Gita 11:36-46
*Arjuna asks Bhagavan's pardon, and pleads with
him to revert to his mortal form.*

Arjuna said,

> *The* universe rightly rejoices and delights
> in your fame, *O* God!
> Demons flee in all directions, terrified.
> All *the* crowds of *the* fulfilled make reverence.
> And why should they not
> revere you, *O* great self,
> greater even than Brahma, *the* original creator?
> *You are the* unending God of gods,
> *the* abode of *the* universe.
> You are imperishable, existent,
> non-existent, *and* that which is beyond.

> You are *the* primal God, *the* breath of ancient times.
> You *are the* highest abode
> of all this universe.
> You *are the* knower, *the* to be known, *the* highest.
> You fill all this universe, *O* you of endless form.
> You are Vayu, Agni, Varuna, *the* Moon;
> Prajapati, and *the* original great-grandfather.
> Reverence, reverence to you *a* thousand times!
> Again, reverence, reverence to you!
> Reverence to you from in front and behind!
> Reverence to you also on all sides, *O* All!

You are unending valor, boundless strength.
You fill all. Therefore, you are all.

If, imagining *you a mere* friend,
saying impetuously,
"O Krishna, O Yadava, O companion,"
from not knowing this majesty of yours,
from confusion, or even with love,
by me to you —
and, as if joking, I disrespected you,
in play, in bed, in sitting down or in eating,
alone, or even before others' eyes,
I ask your pardon for that, *O* Boundless One.

You are *the* father of *the* world,
of *the* animate and inanimate.
You *are* its teacher, to be honored,
greatly venerable, and no other *is* like you.
How could another *be* greater,
even in *the* three worlds, *O* Incomparable Being?

Therefore, bowing in reverence,
prostrating body before you,
I ask pardon of you, *O* Lord to be praised!
Can you be merciful, *O* God, like *a* father to *a* son,
like *a* friend to *a* friend, like *a* lover to *the* beloved?
I am agitated, having seen *the* never before seen.
My mind shakes with fear.
Let me see your *previous* form, *O* God!
Have mercy, *O* God of gods,
abode of *the* universe!

I wish to see you as before,
crowned, armed with *a* club, discus in hand.
Become *again* that four-limbed form,
O you who have all forms!

DISCOURSE NINETEEN
Bhagavad Gita 11:47-49
*Bhagavan assures Arjuna
of the uniqueness of what he has seen.*

Bhagavan said,

I've shown you by my grace, *O* Arjuna,
this highest form: made of brilliance,
universal, unending, primordial —
which no one other than you has seen.
No one in this human world can see my form —
not by scripture, religious work, or study,
not by gifts, ceremonial acts, or fierce austerity —
except you.

Don't tremble, *and* don't be confused,
after seeing my overwhelming form.
See *again* my *finite* form.
Be freed from apprehension,
cheerful in heart, once more.

DISCOURSE TWENTY
Bhagavad Gita 11:52-55
*Bhagavan assures Arjuna that others
will be able to see Him as well.*

Bhagavan said,

You have seen this form,
so hard to see
that even *the* gods long
perpetually to see it.
I can't be seen
as you have seen,
by scripture, or austerity,
or gift, or ritual.
I can be seen in such form
in no other way than by love:
to know and to see, in truth,
and to attain.
Someone doing work in me, depending on me,
loving me, attachment abandoned,
free from hostility toward all *the* living,
comes to me, *O* Pandava.

DISCOURSE TWENTY-ONE
Bhagavad Gita 12:2-20
*Arjuna asks which type of devotee
has better knowledge.*

Bhagavan said,

I consider *the* most devoted
to be people who worship me,
practicing discipline,
minds fixed on me,
endowed with *the* highest faith.
Yet those who honor *the* imperishable,
incomparable, invisible,
all-pervading and thought-surpassing,
unchanging, immovable, *and* constant,
reach me too.
They pacify *the* tumult of *the* senses,
even-minded on all sides,
made content in *the* welfare of all being.
It's a harder road, *though,*
for those who focus on *the* unseen.
Only *a* few of *the* seen
can reach *the* unseen.

Yet, if you worship me,
letting all your works go to me,
intent on me as highest,
not distracted in your practice,
considering me;

I deliver you
from *the* ocean
of death and rebirth.
Let your thoughts live in me.
Keep *your* mind on me alone!
Make *your* intelligence approach me!
Don't doubt you'll live in me
from here onward.

But if you can't keep
your thought steady on me,
try to reach me
by practicing *your* discipline.
If you can't do that, either,
then do my work as *the* highest good.
You'll find me, even if all you can do
is work for my sake.
But if you can't do even that,
then trust my discipline.
Don't sweat *the* work's outcome.
Calm yourself.

Wisdom *is* better than practice.
Meditation *is* superior to wisdom.
Renouncing *the* outcome of work
is better than meditation.
Peace *follows* immediately from renunciation.

I treasure someone who *is*
a non-hater of all *the* living,
a compassionate friend,

free from attachment to things
and building up *an* ego;
stable in pleasure and pain, patient —
a disciplined person, capable of contentment,
self-controlled and values solid,
mind and intelligence fixed on me,
and loving me.

I treasure someone
who doesn't make *the* world afraid,
and who isn't afraid of *the* world.
Such *are* freed from pleasure,
indignation, fear, *and* anxiety.

I treasure someone
who is impartial, pure, *and* able;
sitting apart, free from anxiety;
letting go of undertakings, *and* loving me.

I treasure someone who *is* full of love;
who doesn't rejoice *over success,* or hate *failure*;
doesn't bemoan *the old.* or lust *for the new*;
and can go beyond both pleasure and pain.

I treasure someone who is
even-handed toward enemy and friend,
not shaken in repute and disrepute,
stable in cold and heat, happiness and sorrow,
freed from attachment;
unmoved in blame or praise;
balanced in any circumstance whatsoever;

mind equally open and principled,
full of love.

I treasure tremendously those
who honor *the* words I've spoken here;
who keep *the* faith, intent on me as *the* highest;
and who love me.

DISCOURSE TWENTY-TWO
Bhagavad Gita 13:1-34
*Arjuna asks Bhagavan to explain
the field and the knower of the field.*

Bhagavan said,

> This body is *the* field, they say.
> Those who know claim
> that *the one* knowing
> is *the* knower of *the* field.
> Understand that I
> *am the* knower in all fields.
> When you know *the* field
> and *its* knower, you know me.
>
> Here's my take on
> what this field *is,* and what *its* nature *is;*
> what *its* changes *are*, and from where.
> Who *is* that knower
> and what *is that knower's* power?
> Many have sung about it, many times.
> Seers sing about it
> with various sacred hymns, distinctly,
> the verses holy to the holy ones,
> reasonings full, *and* undeniable.
>
> *The* great elements, consciousness of *an* "I";
> intelligence, *the* unseen;
> eleven senses, five fields
> perceptible to *the* senses;

desire, revulsion, ecstasy, misery,
organism, consciousness, *and* steadiness.
That's how I explain the field, in brief,
with its modifications.

Here are the qualities of those seeking me.
Arrogance and hypocrisy *are* absent.
Non-violence, patience, honesty;
attendance on *the* Teacher, integrity,
stability, self-control;
aversion to *the* objects of sense,
and *an* absence of "I";
keeping in view birth, death,
old age, disease, misery, and wrong;
non-attachment, *a* lack of clinging,
beginning with child, wife, and home;
disciplined equanimity in *the* midst of
desired and undesired outcomes;
trusting in me, and not in another discipline;
loving, not wandering;
frequenting lonely places;
not content among crowds;
constant in awareness of *the* highest;
practicing *the* purpose of truth and wisdom —
this is wisdom, in brief.
Ignorance is what is contrary.

Let me tell you what's to be known.
When you know it, you reach immortality —
the highest brahman, it's said, without beginning;
not being this, *and* not being nothing, either.

This! *It* has hand, foot,
eye, head, and face, everywhere.
It has ears facing all directions in *the* world,
It envelops all.
It takes *the* shape
of *the* basic drives of nature,
yet it's freed from *the* senses.
It's unattached, yet it maintains all.
It's free from *the* basic drives,
yet it experiences them.
It's outside and inside of *the* living.
It's inanimate and animate.
How this can be is beyond subtle.

It's far away and near.
It's undivided among *the* living,
yet as if remaining divided.
This *is the* supporter, *the* devourer,
and *the* creator of *the* living.
This *is the* light of lights,
beyond darkness;
the wisdom, *the* to be known,
the goal of knowledge,
seated in *the* heart of all.

That's *the* field, *the* knowledge,
and *the* to be known, described briefly.
When you love me, when you understand this,
you come near my state of being.
Know nature and *the* breath
to be beginningless also.

Know *that* changes and basic drives
all originate from nature.
The instrument of *the* agent
of *what's* to be done causes material nature.

The fact that you're breathing
is the cause of experiencing pleasure and pain.
Breath, abiding in nature,
experiences nature,
born of *the* basic drives.
Attachment to *the* basic drives causes birth
in *both the* right and *the* wrong wombs.
The highest breath in this body
is said to be *the* highest self.
It is the witness, *the* permitter,
the uplifter, *the one* experiencing, *the* great Lord.
When you understand this breath and nature,
together with *the* basic drives,
you don't have to be born again,
wherever you may be on *life's* journey.

Some figure out self by *the* self,
by meditating on *the* self.
Others figure it out
by *the* discipline of Self-Realization,
and others by *the* discipline of work.
Some can't figure it out, but they can
worship, hearing about it from others.
They go beyond death, too,
because they love what they've heard.

Understand that any being whatsoever —
animate or inanimate —
is born from *the* union
of *the* field and *its* knower.

When you see *the* highest Lord
existing alike in all *the* living,
not dying when they die,
you truly see.
When you *train yourself to* see
the same Lord, established on all sides,
you don't injure self by *the* self.
From there, you reach *the* highest path.
When you can see work
as being done entirely by nature,
and no longer fixate on yourself as *the* doer,
you truly see.
When you can see *the* various
states of being abiding in one,
and spreading out from there,
you're not far from brahman.

This eternal highest Self
has no beginning. *The* basic drives *are* absent.
It does not act. *It* is not polluted,
even living in *a* body.
Just as space cannot be polluted
by *the* objects it contains,
the self cannot be polluted
in *the* body, either.

As *the* Sun, by itself,
lights up this entire world,
so *the* knower of *the* field
lights up *the* entire field.

When you genuinely understand
the relationship between *the* field
and *the* knower of *the* field;
and how *the* living *are* freed from nature,
you go to *the* highest.

DISCOURSE TWENTY-THREE
Bhagavad Gita 14:1-20
*Bhagavan expounds on the three basic drives
that define material existence.*

Bhagavan said,

>Let me explain again,
>to be sure you understand it.
>*The* best thing, *the* highest wisdom,
>is whatever drives you to *the* ultimate.
>Depend on this wisdom,
>and come to full communion with me.
>Those who do so are not born, even at creation,
>and do not shake at dissolution.
>
>I put *the* seed in this,
>in great brahman's womb.
>*The* origin of all *the* living
>starts there.
>Brahman is *the* womb.
>I *am the* seed-sowing father.
>All wombs come to be
>in brahman.
>
>Light, power, darkness,
>*the* three basic drives of nature,
>chain *the* eternal embodied *one*
>in *a* body.
>Even brilliant light,
>free from impurity, free from disease,

binds people to positive sensations,
by attachment to wisdom.
Understand power, characterized by passion,
born from thirst and attachment!
This chains *the* embodied *one*
by attachment to work.
Understand darkness, born of ignorance,
the confusion of all embodied *ones*!
This chains by distraction,
laziness, and sleep.

Light causes *an* attachment to happiness.
Power causes *an* attachment to work.
Darkness veils wisdom,
and causes *an* attachment to confusion.

Light comes to be *when it* prevails
over power and darkness;
power *when it prevails*
over light and darkness;
darkness *when it prevails*
over light and power.
When wisdom can be known,
light *is* dominant.
A brightness is born
in all this body's gates.
When power is dominant,
greed, exertion,
the starting of actions,
restlessness, *and* lust, are born.

When darkness is dominant,
dullness, lack of exertion,
negligence, *and* confusion
are born.

When *an* embodied *one*
goes to dissolution with light dominant,
that person arrives at *the* pure worlds,
of those who know *the* highest.
If you go to dissolution with power dominant,
you're born among those attached to work.
Likewise, if you go in darkness,
you go to *the* wombs of *the* confused.

Light, without impurity, is t*he* outcome
of work well-performed, they say.
Power produces pain.
Darkness yields ignorance.
Wisdom is born from light,
and lust from power.
Negligence and confusion bubble up
from darkness, as does ignorance.
Those established in light go upward.
Those pursuing power stay in *the* middle.
Those remaining in *the* lowest drive,
darkness, go downward.

When you look, and see no doer
other than *the* three basic drives,
and you know *one* higher than *the* basic drives,
you come to my being.

An embodied *self*, going beyond
a body originating in these three basic drives,
finds immortality, released
from birth, death, old age, and misery.

DISCOURSE TWENTY-FOUR
Bhagavad Gita 14:22-27
*Arjuna asks Bhagavan to explain
how to recognize one who has gone beyond
the basic drives of nature.*

Bhagavan said,

>They'll neither hate *the* occurrences,
nor desire *the* non-occurrences
of brightness, or progress,
or confusion.
They remain as if sitting apart,
not shaken by *the* three basic drives.
"Basic drives move all this," *they think.*
They stand firm. They don't waver.

>They're *the* same in pleasure and in pain,
self-reliant. Dirt, stone, and gold
are *the* same to them. *The* loved
and *the* unloved *are* equal. They're steady.
Blame and praise *are* equal.
They're the same in repute and disrepute;
the same toward factions of friend and enemy.
Giving up all beginnings, those people, it's said,
go beyond *the* basic drives.

>When you obey me
with unwavering, disciplined love,
you, too, go beyond these three basic drives,
ready for absorption in brahman.

I am *the* basis of brahman,
of *the* undying and eternal,
of perpetual righteousness,
and of absolute bliss.

DISCOURSE TWENTY-FIVE
Bhagavad Gita 15:1-20
Arjuna asks how best to know Bhagavan.

Bhagavan said,

The Asvattha tree, they say, *is* imperishable.
Its root *is* high, *its* branches low.
Its leaves are hymns.
Who knows it is *a* knower of scripture.
Wide-spreading branches, low and high,
are nurtured by basic drives.
Its shoots *are* born of sense objects,
and its roots, stretched out below,
engender work in *the* human world.
Its form isn't perceptible here on earth:
not *its* end, not *its* beginning, and not *its* continuing.
Cut down this tree, whose roots are fully grown,
by *the* strong ax of non-attachment!

From there, seek that place which,
once reached, you don't have to return again.
I take refuge in that primal breath,
from which activity flowed in ancient times.
Without arrogance or confusion,
attachment to wrongs overcome,
abide in *the* original self, desires turned away.
This frees you from *the* dualities
known as pleasure and pain.

This highest abode is mine,
not that *abode which the* Sun illumines,
or *the* moon, or flame.
Once seekers have gone there,
they don't turn back.
A mere fraction of me
becomes *a* primordial self.
It drags *with it the* mind
and the six senses, abiding in nature.

When *the* Lord acquires
a body, and when it departs *from one*,
it goes holding on to these,
like *a* wind taking scents from *a* place of refuge.
This *fractional self* enjoys *the* objects of sense,
and presides over hearing,
sight, touch, taste, smell,
and *the* mind.
The confused don't perceive *it*,
whether departing or remaining,
whether enjoying or *just* accompanied
by *the* basic drives.
Those with wisdom's eye do perceive.
The disciplined perceive this,
abiding in *the* self.
Unprepared, thoughtless selves
don't perceive it, though they strive *for it*.

A brilliance excelling *the* Sun
illumines *the* universe completely.

Know that brilliance to be mine,
which is in *the* Moon and which is in fire.
I support with power
all *the* living entering *the* earth.
I cause all plants to thrive,
becoming soma, juicy-selved.
I become *the* digestive fire in all people,
entering *the* body of breathing beings.
Joined to vital breath and abdominal breath,
I digest *the* four kinds of food.
I sit in *the* heart of all.
Memory, wisdom, and reasoning *arise* from me.
I am to be known from all scriptures.
I fulfill both scripture and *the* knower of scripture.

These two breaths, perishable
and imperishable, are in *the* world.
All *the* living are perishable.
The imperishable is called unchanging.
The highest breath is something else,
called *the* highest self,
the eternal Lord, who, coming into
the three worlds, bears them.
Since I go beyond
perishable and imperishable,
celebrate me as *the* highest breath,
in *the* world and in scripture.

When you know me in this way
as *the* highest breath, *you're* no longer confused,

Knowing all, love me
with *the* whole being.
I proclaim this most secret teaching,
O Blameless One.
Someone who is wise, knowing this,
can be enlightened, with all duties fulfilled.

DISCOURSE TWENTY-SIX
Bhagavad Gita 16:1-24
*Bhagavan describes the mark
of divine and demonic beings.*

Bhagavan said,

> Fear *is* absent and being *is* pure
> in those influenced by *the* divine.
> They abide in disciplined wisdom,
> giving, self-control, and religious work;
> repeating holy words to themselves;
> austere *and* upright.
> *They are* non-violent *and* truth telling.
> Anger *is* absent. Renunciation
> *and* peace *are present.*
> Slander *is* absent. Compassion
> for *the* living *is present.*
> Freed from lust,
> vigorous, patient, courageous,
> clean *in body and mind*,
> hatred absent, and not overly proud —
> these are divinity's endowment
> among *the* born.
>
> *The* demonic endowment includes
> hypocrisy, arrogance, conceit,
> anger, foul language,
> and well-born ignorance.
> *The* divine endowment leads to liberation.
> *The* demonic thought *leads* to chains.

Don't grieve! You are born
to *the* divine endowment.

Two types of beings exist
in this world: divine and demonic.
I've explained *the* divine in detail.
Hear about *the* demonic from me *directly*.
Demonic people don't understand
activity and inactivity.
When you look at them, you find
neither cleanliness *of body and mind*,
nor good conduct, nor even truth.
"This *is a* universe without god,
without truth, without solid ground," they say,
"not one created by another."
What else? "*All this is* caused by lust."

Holding this view, they
lose themselves, intelligence stunted.
With cruel works, they come forth *as* enemies,
bent on *the* destruction of *the* world.
They go on, making impure promises;
attached to want, hard to fill;
attended by hypocrisy, pride, and lust;
accepting false information from confusion,
attached to immeasurable anxiety
ending in death,
holding gratification of desire as *the* highest aim,
having no doubt, so much so —
chained by *a* hundred false hopes,
devoted to lust and anger,

they want only to satisfy their lust,
and pile up riches by unjust means.
"I acquired this today.
I'll get that tomorrow.
This *is* mine. All this wealth
will be *mine* again.
I destroyed that enemy,
and I will destroy others also.
I *am the* Lord. I *am the* enjoyer.
I *am* successful. I *am* powerful and happy.
I am wealthy *and* high-born.
What other is like me? Now, I'll do
religious work and charity, and be happy."

Ignorance confuses them.
Carried away by not *a* few imaginings,
covered in *a* trap of confusion,
clinging to *the* gratification of desire,
they fall into *an* impure hell.
Conceited, stubborn, obsessed
by wealth; proud, and arrogant,
they worship in name only, with works
of hypocrisy, not according to rule.
Clinging to ego, force,
arrogance, lust, and anger,
the envious hate me,
in their own and in others' bodies.

I hurl those who hate,
those who are cruel, *the* vile,
into perpetual cycles of rebirth,

and into demonic wombs.
The confused,
entering demonic wombs,
not reaching me in birth after birth,
go from there to *the* lowest path.

The three-fold gate of hell,
destructive of self,
is lust, anger, and greed.
Give up those three, Arjuna!
You do best for yourself
when you're released
from these three gates of darkness.
From there, it's *a* short step to *the* highest path.
But if you ignore what scripture teaches,
and follow *the* lead of lust,
you can't reach fulfillment,
or happiness, or *the* highest path.

Determine *the* scriptural standard for yourself —
what's to be done, and *what's* not to be done.
When you're aware of what scripture requires,
you can work here in *the* world.

DISCOURSE TWENTY-SEVEN
Bhagavad Gita 17:2-28
*Arjuna asks about faith, and those who
do religious works differently.*

Bhagavan said,

Understand this.
There are three kinds of faith.
Faith is born of innate nature.
It's either of light, of power, or of darkness.
Faith is following
the light of each.
A human is made of faith.
As someone's faith *is*, so are they.
Those in light do religious works for *the* divine.
Those in power do them for spirits and demons.
Those in darkness do them
for *the* dead, for ghosts, *and* for *the* worst.

Living humans suffer anguish
that scripture never commands,
yoked to fraud and ego,
with lust, anger, and force.
Understand that they're living
like demons, mindlessly torturing
the aggregates of being in *the* body;
and me, as well, within *the* body.

Here are the three kinds
of preferred food:

religious work, austerity, and charity.
Understand *the* differentiation among them.
Foods dear to those pursuing light,
promoting life, truth, strength, health,
happiness, and satisfaction,
are savory, smooth, solid, and pleasant.
Those devoted to power want food
that is pungent, sour, salty, excessively hot,
fiery, rough, and scorching —
causing pain, sorrow, and sickness.
Food dear to those intent on darkness
is stale, tasteless,
rotten, and left-over,
which *is* rejected and impure.

Religious work which is offered by those
not attached to outcome *is* scripturally observant.
The mind *is* concentrated only this way.
This is *the offering of* those focused on light.
That which *is* offered
with outcome in mind,
and with *a* hypocritical purpose,
is *the offering of* those devoted to power.
Understand that food not offered,
scripture neglected, *the* holy word left out,
fees not paid, *are* religious works
of those focused on darkness.

Bodily austerity is said to be
chaste and non-violent
in those reverencing *the* divine,

the born again, *true* teachers, and *the* wise,
Austerity of speech is said to be
the practice of *a* word not causing distress,
which is true, agreeable, and wholesome;
and repeating holy words to oneself.
Austerity of mind gives rise
to peace of mind, gentleness,
silence, self-control,
and purity of being.
People regard *what is* undergone
with *the* highest faith as characterized by light.
The disciplined perform this three-fold austerity,
not desiring *an* outcome.

I declare austerity which is performed
with hypocrisy here on earth,
merely to win honor, respect, and reverence,
to be power-driven, unsteady, *and* impermanent.
Austerity performed
with confused notions of self, with torment,
or with *the* aim of destroying another,
is mired in darkness.

The best gift is one you give
at the proper place and time
and to *a* deserving person;
to someone you don't owe *a* favor.
That gift is rooted in light.
A gift given
for *the* sake of reward,
or hoping to manipulate *an* outcome,

or grudgingly, *is* driven by power.
A gift given at *the* wrong place and time,
to those who don't deserve it,
without paying respect, with contempt,
belongs to darkness.

Brahman's three-fold command
says, "**This Oṁ** *is* **Truth**,"
ordaining from of old
seekers, scriptures, and religious works.
Because of this, brahman's speakers
begin religious work, austerity,
and charity, chanting *the* **Oṁ**,
as set forth in precepts.
By saying **This**, not aiming
at *an* outcome, seekers of liberation
do acts of worship and austerity,
and charitable works of various sorts.
This designates reality,
and good intention.
The sound of **This** is used
in praiseworthy work.
Steadfast **Truth** is spoken
in religious work, austerity, and charity.
Work serving that purpose
is designated as **Truth**.

Falsehood is *an* offering made,
or *an* austerity practiced,
without faith. It is nothing to us,
hereafter or here.

DISCOURSE TWENTY-EIGHT
Bhagavad Gita 18:2-72
Arjuna asks Bhagavan to explain renunciation.

Bhagavan said,

Poets understand renunciation
as letting go of works driven by lust.
The clear-eyed say renunciation
is the abandonment of all outcome.
Some wise *teachers* say work
is full of evil, and thus to be given up.
Others say that *the* work of worship, charity,
and austerity is not to be given up.

I've concluded this
about renunciation.
There are three ways *of giving things up*,
of renunciation.
Don't give up *the* work
of worship, charity, and austerity,
Do it! Religious work, charity, and austerity
purify *the* wise.
Do these works, giving up
attachment and outcome.
Those kinds of work are *the* best ways
of renunciation, in my opinion.
Don't give up doing what you have to do.
That won't work for you.
Giving that up would be confusion.
Stay out of *the* dark with that.

If you renounce work just because it's hard,
or because you're afraid of discomfort,
that's power-driven. You won't magically
reach what you imagine *renunciation* to be.
Whatever work *you* have to do,
do *in a* disciplined *manner*.
That's *the* sort of renunciation,
of letting go, that casts light.

If your renunciation is filled
with goodness, if your doubt *is* cut away,
you manage not to hate *the* disagreeable,
or hold too tight to *the* agreeable.
Those in *a* body
can't give up work entirely.
A renunciate gives up
the outcome of work.

Consequences reach us three ways
when we die, if we're still attached:
by what y*ou* don't want, by what you do want,
and by *a* mixture of *the* two.
A renunciate doesn't need *a specific* outcome.

I've seen five causes
repeat themselves, all my life,
keys to success in everything,
spelled out in Self-Realization:
the basis; *the* doer;
the various sorts of means;
the distinct activities;

and the divine. In this case, *it's the* fifth.

I've seen five origins, too,
whatever work someone starts:
whether by body, speech, or mind,
whether in favor or against.
People who see themselves
as *the* only ones working
don't quite see everything.
Fools don't see at all.
Is there someone whose wits
aren't puffed up or defiled,
who isn't bound, even after
wasting these worlds?

Wisdom, *the* to be known, the knower,
are the three-fold motivations to work.
The means, *the* task itself, *and the* agent,
are the three-fold constituents of work.

Wisdom, work, and worker *are*
three-fold, too: determined by *the* basic drives,
in *the* overall reckoning of *the* basic drives.
Understand them, too.
Wisdom that gives you *the* ability
to see one, undivided,
eternal being in all *the* living,
comes from light.
Wisdom which knows
all *the* living *as* various beings
of different species, individually,

comes from power.
Something fixated on one issue,
as if nothing else mattered, unconcerned
with reasoning, without real purpose, trivial,
comes from darkness.
When your work is disciplined,
freed from attachment, done without
lust or hatred, not looking for *a* hidden outcome,
it's done in light.
Work done with much effort,
lusting after *the* lusts themselves,
benefiting *the* worker and no one else,
is driven by power.
Work started in confusion,
refusing to notice *an* inevitable outcome,
causing loss, violence, carelessness,
and injury to others,
seeps out of darkness.

You're in *the* light when you're
freed from attachment; freed from self-puffery;
when you can live with courage and determination,
undisturbed in success or failure.
It's all about power when
you lust passionately for *an* outcome,
greedy, violent, *and* impure.
It leads to *the* heights and *the* depths.
When you do works that *are* undisciplined,
vulgar, obstinate, deceitful, vile, *and* lazy,
despondent and procrastinating,
such *works* slouch out of darkness.

Understand intelligence
and steadfastness as three-fold,
according to *the* basic drives.
I'll tell you all about it, if you'll listen.
The kind of intelligence that knows
activity and inactivity; what's to be done
and what's not; what's to be feared
and what isn't; slavery and freedom —
is from light.
Intelligence that chooses incorrectly
between righteousness and unrighteousness,
what's to be done and what isn't. —
is about power.
Understanding that imagines
wrong as right, wrapped in gloom,
all *its* aims backwards,
spills out of darkness.

Use mind, breath, and senses,
disciplined by ongoing practice,
to find that steadiness
which is born of light.
But lusting for *an* outcome
that lets you hold on to
duty, desire, and wealth,
yields *a* steadiness only of power.
When *the* dimwitted refuse
to give up sleep, fear, sorrow,
depression, and pride,
it's a steadfastness of darkness.

Understand *a* three-fold happiness too,
since *a* lot of this has been heavy.
You learn to enjoy it by practice,
and go on from there to *the* end of suffering.
There's a happiness born of light that,
at *the* start, may taste like poison.
When it matures, though, it's sweet wine.
Such *is* born from *the* clarity of your own soul.
The happiness born from *the* contact of sense
with sense object may taste like sweet wine
at the start, but when it matures it's poison.
That kind is born out of power.
There's even *a* happiness which confuses *the* self,
from *the* beginning through *the* inevitable
consequences. *It bubbles up* from sleep, idleness,
and negligence. That kind comes from darkness.

No existence born of nature, either
on earth or in heaven among gods,
can exist free from
the three basic drives.
The basic drives,
innate in nature, distribute
t*he* works of priests, warriors,
farmers and traders, and laborers,
The works of priests, born of innate nature,
*include t*ranquility, restraint, austerity,
cleanliness, patience, honesty,
wisdom, discernment, *and* belief in God.
The work of warriors, born of innate nature,
includes heroism, majesty, courage, skill —

even *that of* not running away in battle —
generosity, and nobility of spirit,
The work of farmers and traders, born
of innate nature, includes agriculture,
raising animals, *and* commerce.
Laborers are born of nature to serve.

Find fulfillment
in your own repeated duty.
Let me tell you how
that can happen.
You find fulfillment
doing your own work,
consciously loving *the* Origin of all *the* living,
who pervades all this.
You're better off doing your own duty, even if you
can't finish it, than finishing someone else's.
You don't pile up guilt doing *the* work
your own nature prescribes.
Don't give up your innate work,
even if you can't finish it.
All beginnings are unfinished,
just as all fire produces smoke.

Some reach intelligence by renunciation,
not attached on any side,
pacified in self *and* lust overcome.
That's the highest completion of work.
I've also seen that,
once you learn to be content,
you learn to live near brahman as well.

That is wisdom's highest state.
Joined with pure intelligence;
self-control steady;
sense objects given up, beginning with sound;
setting aside passion and hatred;
living apart, eating lightly;
speech, body, and mind controlled;
devoted continually to disciplined meditation;
taking refuge in dispassion;
giving up ego, force,
arrogance, longing, anger, and possession;
not acquisitive, at peace;
you are fit for oneness with brahman.

When you're one with brahman,
at peace in *your* own self, you don't have to mourn,
y*ou* don't have to want *things*,
and you can be impartial among all *the* living.
You also find pure love for me.
Some come to know who I am,
even how great I am, by love for me.
Since they know me in reality,
they commune with me immediately.
They find my kindness,
my eternal, unchanging abode,
trusting me, continually,
doing all works.

Keep *your* mind on me, Arjuna.
Let all works go to me.
Love me as *the* highest in *your* thought.

Take refuge in disciplined intelligence.
You'll get beyond life's rough goings
by my grace, with *your* mind on me.
But if you won't listen
because of ego, you'll perish.

If you imagine, "I will not fight,"
depending on *your own* ego,
it won't work out that way.
Nature will force you.
You'll end up doing what you don't want,
from confusion, bound by
your own nature, your own work,
even against *your* will.

The Lord of all *the* living
stands in *the* heart, *O* Arjuna,
causing all *the* living to move
on *a* mechanism of illusion.
Go to that Lord alone,
with *your* whole being.
Reach *the* highest peace,
an eternal abode, by that grace

But think about what I've told you.
This wisdom is more secret than secret,
and I've told it to you, well enough.
Now, do what you choose.

But understand *the* highest word
the most secret of all secrets:

I genuinely love you,
and I will speak your good.
Fix your mind on me. Love me.
Do religious work for me. Reverence me.
That way you'll come to me in truth.
I promise you are dear to me.
Set aside all gimmicks,
and take refuge in me alone!
I will release you from
all wrongs. Don't grieve.

My message isn't for someone
who won't practice austerity.
It's never for someone who won't love!
It's not for *those* who won't listen,
or *those* who speak evil of me.
Those who open this highest secret
to others who love me,
perform *the* highest love for me.
They'll come to me, without doubt.
No one will be dearer to me
than they will be;
No other on earth
will be dearer to me.

If someone merely recites
this holy conversation of ours,
I'll have been loved, in my opinion,
by *the* wisdom they offered.
If someone merely hears, full of faith,
not scoffing, they'll be set free, too,

to reach *the* pure, happy worlds
of those whose works are pure.

Have you paid attention
to me, Arjuna?
Has this cleared up
confusion and ignorance?

Arjuna Answers Bhagavan's Closing Questions
Bhagavad Gita 18:73

Arjuna said,

> I'm standing. You've destroyed my confusion.
> I will remember, and my doubt is gone.
> By your grace to me, *O* Unchanging *One,*
> I will do what you command.

(The End of Bhagavan's Song)

Excerpts from
ऋग्वेद
Rig Veda

The Well-spoken Hymn of Not Non-existence.

Neither non-existence nor existence existed then,
neither space nor sky beyond existed at all.
Death was not, then, nor immortality,
nor, then, was light by day or by night.
Without breath, that *one* was there
by its own power.
Beyond, apart from that, was nothing at all.

Darkness was enveloped in darkness
at *the* beginning.
All this *was* unmanifested water.
That abyss was concealed by *the* void.
By great heat one was born.

Longing arose first;
then, *the* creative impulse upon *the* mind,
which was foremost.
The wise found *the* bond of existence
in non-existence,
by deep reflection in *the* heart.
A beam of light was spread out across these.
Was it possibly below or above?

Seed-bearers were *there*,
majestic beings were *there* —
power below, effort above.

Who truly knows?
Who in this world could openly declare
from where this creation arose?
The gods came later, after this creation.
Who knows from where it has arisen?
From where, indeed, *came*
the creation thereafter —
by fashioning or not?
He who is overseer of this in *the* highest height,
he, indeed, knows if, or he does not know.

नासदीय सूक्त
Nāsadīya Sūkta
ऋग्वेद
Rig Veda 10:129:1-7

Excerpts from
उपनिषद्
The Upanishads

"The Straight Translation"
of *Isha Upanishad*

Whatever moves in *the* world, even *the* smallest,
all this *is* filled by God.
By what has been abandoned, enjoy!
Do not covet! Whose wealth *is it,* indeed?

Working here,
one might live *a* hundred years.
It exists so in no other way for you;
work does not endure for humanity.

Those godless worlds
are covered with blinding darkness.
Whoever among them destroys their own self
goes to those worlds after death.

Unmoving, *it is* swifter than mind;
the gods did not reach *it* before it soared away.
That, though standing *still*,
goes beyond others running.
Mātariśvā (Breathes-in-the-Mother)
establishes waters.

That moves, that does not move, far and near —
That *is* inside of everything.
That *is* outside of everything.

Someone who perceives
all *the* living in *the* self,
and *the* self in all *the* living,
as *a* result, does not despise.
In whom, for one who knows,
self itself has become all *the* living,
what confusion *remains* there, what sorrow,
for one who sees oneness?

The one filled all, luminous,
without body, without blemish,
without sinews, pure, unpierced by evil.
Self-existent in truth, it arranged
purposes for eternal ages.

They enter into blind darkness
who sit near ignorance.
From that, as if into greater darkness,
enter those devoted to knowledge.
One thing, they said,
comes by means of knowledge.
Another, they said, *comes* by means of ignorance.
Thus we have heard from *the* wise
who have explained that to us.
Whoever knows
both knowledge and ignorance together,
transcending death through ignorance,

attains immortality through knowledge.

They fall into blind darkness
who devote themselves to nothingness.
They fall into even deeper darkness
who are attached to manifestation.
One thing, they said,
results from manifestation,
and another from nothingness.
Thus we have heard from *the* wise
who have explained that to us.
Whoever knows
manifestation and dissolution both together,
transcending death through dissolution,
attains immortality through manifestation.

Truth's face is covered by *a* golden mask.
You, O Sun, uncover that by truth,
that one may see!
O Nourisher, solitary seer, O Yama,
O Sun of creation's Lord,
spread apart your rays, withdraw!
That radiant Person whose transcendent form
I see, that very one —
I am he.

Breath enters immortal breath,
then this body ends in ashes.
Oṁ. *O* Understanding, remember past actions!
Remember, *O* Understanding!
Remember past actions!"

O Agni, lead us all by *the* good path to well-being,
O Divine One, knower of wisdom,
drive away from us *the* harmful force
of wrongdoing!
We offer words of praise, reverence, to you.

ईशोपनिषत्
Isha Upanishad 1:1-18

Translator's Notes

1. **Various substitutions used for common Sanskrit terms.**

Bhagavān:
The Sanskrit root word in *Bhagavan* means to love, to partake, to share; and implies limitless fullness.

Gunas: three basic drives of material nature.
The drives are believed to be innate in material nature. In Sanskrit, the terms are *sattva*, *rajas*, and *tamas*. I have translated them as "light," "power," and "darkness," respectively, in an effort to make them clearer to readers outside of South Asia.

Karma/Akarma: work/idleness

Prakriti: material nature, as explored in Self-Realization.

Purusha: breath, spirit, uncovered in Self-Realization; not of material nature; the highest Human, revealed in the text to be divine; see Genesis 2:7 in reference to the use of "breath."

Sāṅkhye: Self-Realization; one of the seven major philosophical movements in formative South Asian thought, whose methods Bhagavan teaches freely in ***Bhagavad Gita***.

Vedas: scriptures.

Yajña: religious work, religious offering.

Yoga: discipline.
For many Westerners, *yoga* means stretching and exercise. For some, suspicious of its Hindu roots, it is something darker. The Sanskrit root links to the word "yoke," the means by which a draft animal is harnessed to work, in contrast to its natural inclination. Thus, yoga is a discipline. Yes, exercise and stretching are a discipline, but they're hardly all discipline. Bhagavan assumes the importance of discipline in any work, and urges Arjuna to practice it.

The "nine-gated city" is the human body; its nine "gates" are two eyes, two ears, two nostrils, one mouth, one opening for excretion, and one for procreation.

The words are defined this way to help with readability, not to obscure the complexity of the original Sanskrit terms.

2. Passive Voice and Third-Person Statements
As is often the case in ancient wisdom literature, ***Bhagavad Gita*** uses passive voice constructions (e. g., "the wisdom is given by me...") and third-person constructions (e. g., "one may obtain...").

I have in general changed the passive voice to active voice (e. g., "I give you wisdom..."), and third-person constructions to second-person (e. g., "YOU may attain...")

These changes make the dialogue more direct, as if a wise elder is addressing a younger seeker. Bhagavan in the poem is God embodied, and his language deserves to be lofty. Yet he also loves Arjuna, and wishes for him well-being and understanding.

I hope the changes in construction help clarify both those emphases at once.

3. "Stained glass" language.
As I found to be the case when I translated ***The Bible***, there's a depth to the text that comes out when it is stripped of its "stained glass" language. "Stained glass" language is flowery prose and untranslated terms that make the text sound more like what proper religious folks think it ought to.

Bhagavan, who does most of the singing in this "Song of God," says a lot about the importance of sacrifice. In the context of ***Mahabharata***, sacrifice meant worshiping the holy in the manner prescribed in the earliest ***Vedas***, the most ancient of which are now considered Hindu scriptures.

I offer in place of "sacrifice" the phrase "religious work," since most of us will not be offering Vedic sacrifices according to ancient ritual any time soon.

This is how I understand it. Religious work is anything we do voluntarily, for the holy, or for others, or for both. We do not have to do it. We are invited to do it.

What we spend our free time doing reflects what we actually value, and what we don't. Doing religious work forms a sense of the holy in and among us. Bhagavan considered such work vital on many levels.

Bhagavan quotes Patanjali, the first human in South Asian myth, as teaching that human beings were created alongside religious works. Religious work is essential not simply to who we are, but more importantly, to who we become.

Bhagavan says that when we perform such work, for the holy, for others, or for both, we, in effect, bring about that holy order which sees beyond the purely selfish. As we do so, we find that the holy, unselfish order brings us into being as well. It's a self-reinforcing reality.

What sort of world do we imagine and work for?

If doing so is "works righteousness," as some might say, it is so in a peculiarly gracious way. The possibility of such an order is revealed by grace.

Bhagavan tells us that **not to participate** in this sort of religious work, **not to help** turn the wheel of mercy and compassion among us, is theft.

Religious work may vary from setting to setting, place to place. One size need not fit all. Feed a hungry person. Pause a moment to reflect on the mystery of life. Worship. Participate, in your own way, in an order vastly larger than most of us realize.

It is, of course, long tradition to do religious work on a Sabbath eve, or a Sunday morning. Whatever time we choose, though, whatever form our religious work takes, Bhagavan advises that we do better for ourselves — we do our duty — in doing so.

4. A Backstory of Arjuna and Krishna
Arjuna and Krishna have a backstory in *Mahabharata*. Krishna had won his kingdom in battle, and later joined

Arjuna against a common enemy. So successful had they been together, that they were considered invincible.

When war broke out over the royal succession in Kurukshetra, Arjuna turned to Krishna for help. Yet Krishna had made a vow that precluded him from fighting.

Krishna was a person of his word, yet he also loved Arjuna, and this was Arjuna's moment of desperate need.

At that point, Krishna gave Arjuna a choice. Krishna could accompany him alone, keeping his vow not to fight. Or Krishna could send in his place his army of 50,000, fully armed and ready to fight, under Arjuna's command. In that scenario, though, Krishna would not accompany Arjuna.

Arjuna chose Krishna alone, rather than an army of 50,000. Such was the immediate context of ***Bhagavad Gita.***

6. "What's with All the Italics?"

In the tradition of the translators of the *Authorized Version* of the English Bible, the *"King James" Version,* when I have to add a word in English that does not appear in Sanskrit, I put the word in italics

As in Latin, Sanskrit has no definite or indefinite articles, no equivalents to the English words, "the," "a," or "an." Forms of the "to be" verb are often left out, as well. All such words are added to the text in italics.

7. Where Did All the Nicknames Go?

Krishna and Arjuna address each other in the ancient text with multiple nicknames, called "epithets" in scholarly circles. Such epithets usually express a relationship. Krishna, for instance, calls Arjuna, "Partha," "Pandava," "Conqueror of Wealth," and "Mighty-Limbed One," among others.

I removed most of them from the translation, and occasionally replaced them with a proper name. The epithets flow in the rhythm of Sanskrit poetry, but tend to clog the flow in English, at least from my ****Discount Mystic**** perspective.

Bhagavan addresses Arjuna, a biological male, as a beloved friend during a terrifying crisis the latter must face.

ALSO BY THE AUTHOR

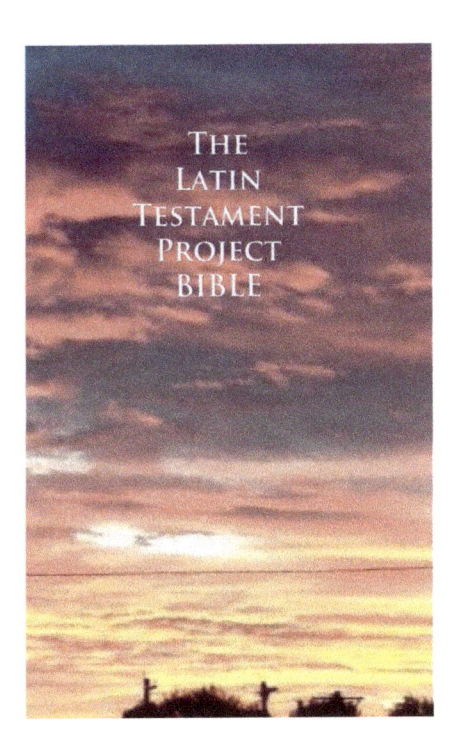

The Latin Testament Project Bible

Translated by John Cunyus
ISBN: 978-1936497294

The Latin Testament Project Bible (LTPB) translates ***The Vulgate***, the Latin language version of the Bible constructed by Saint Jerome between 382 and 405 AD. The **LTPB** contains the Old and New Testaments, and the Apocrypha. The print book is color-coded, for ease of study.

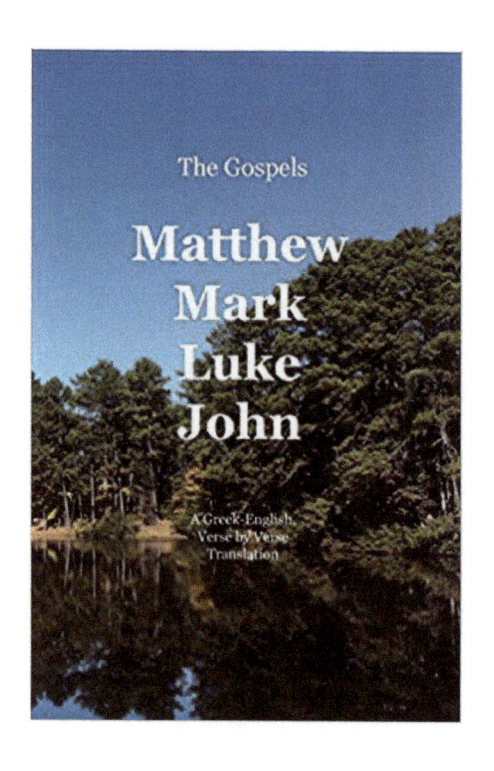

The Gospels:
Matthew, Mark, Luke, John
(A Greek-English, Verse by Verse Translation)

Translated by John G. Cunyus
ISBN: 978-1936497-35-5

This book presents the Christian Gospels, Matthew, Mark, Luke, and John, in a color-coded, Greek-English, verse by verse format. Each verse of the original Greek is followed by its English translation. The work also includes brief guidelines for language instructors, and detailed outlines of the Gospels themselves.

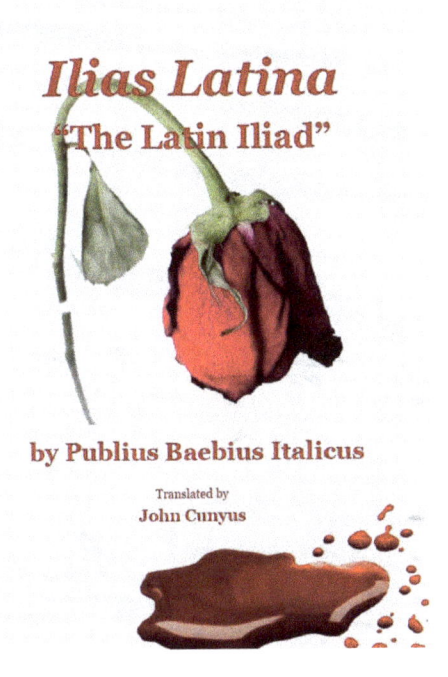

Ilias Latina
"The Latin Iliad"

by Publius Baebius Italicus

Translated by
John Cunyus

Ilias Latina
"The Latin Iliad"

by Publius Baebius Italicus,
translated by John Cunyus.

Ilias Latina (The Latin Iliad) is a condensed version of *The Iliad*, by Homer. This version contains both a Latin-English, and an English-only version of the ancient poem. It can be useful for someone who wants to study Latin, or who just wants to enjoy a new English version of a very old work.

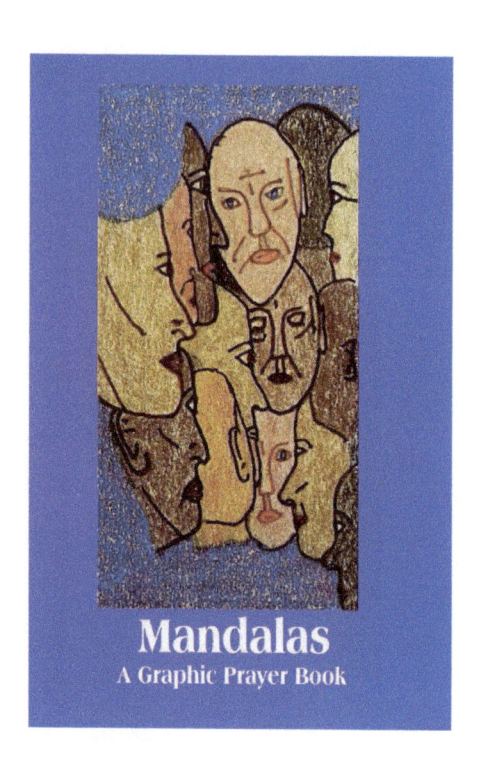

Mandalas
A Graphic Prayer Book

By John G. Cunyus
ISBN: 978-1-936497-43-0

("Graphic" means "Illustrated.")

Mandalas: A Graphic Prayer Book is a collection of drawings and meditations. It is written to broaden and deepen the reader's spiritual life and growth. The work explores significant themes from the Bible as well as insights from South Asian theologians.

The Liberty Tree:
One Hundred Faces of America
(An Illustrated History)

by John Cunyus
ISBN: 978-1-936497-47-1

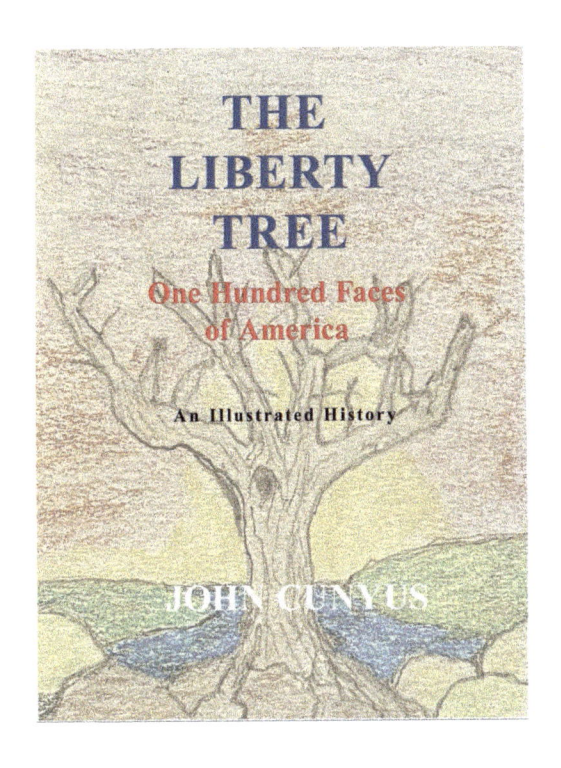

The Liberty Tree: One Hundred Faces of America, is an illustrated history of Liberty in America. Liberty, in turn, is the ability to make our own life decisions according to our own sense of what is best. This book tells the story of Liberty in America through profiles of one hundred Americans.

Bhagavan's Song
The Dialogues of
Krishna and Arjuna
Translated by John G. Cunyus.

Imagine that all of reality—
God and creation,
the living, the dead, and the yet to live,
the visible and the invisible—

took a form that wouldn't fry you like a bug-zapper,
and met you at the brink of your life's greatest trial.

Arjuna faces a terrible decision he can't postpone.

Bhagavan answers his questions—and offers him counsel.

If you've ever stood at such a crossroads,
Bhagavan may be singing to you.

This volume includes:
Bhagavan's Song,
The Texas Isha,
Rig Veda's "Well-Spoken Hymn"...
and more.

**SEARCHLIGHT PRESS
DALLAS, TEXAS**

About the Translator

John G. Cunyus is a retired Christian pastor. He holds a degree in History and Religious Studies from Rice University, and is the translator of *The Latin Testament Project Bible*, a completely new edition of the Latin Vulgate Bible. His most recent work is *The Liberty Tree: One Hundred Faces of America.*

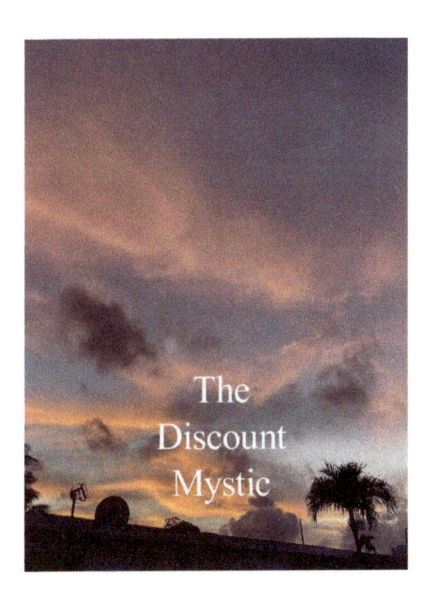

Searchlight Press
****The Discount Mystic****
"Ancient Wisdom. Texas Twang."
www.JohnCunyus.com
5634 Ledgestone Drive
Dallas, TX. 75214-2026